The Change¹⁸

Insights into Self-Empowerment

Jim Britt ~ Jim Lutes

With

Co-authors From Around the World

The Change[18]

Jim Britt ~ Jim Lutes

All Rights Reserved

Copyright 2023
The Change
10556 Combie Road, Suite 6205
Auburn, CA 95602

The use of any part of this publication, whether reproduced, stored in any retrieval system or transmitted in any forms or by any means, electronic or otherwise, without the prior written consent of the publisher, is an infringement of copyright law.

Jim Lutes ~ Jim Britt

The Change

ISBN#

Co-authors

Jonathan Amundsen

Anoushiravan Khaze'

Stacie Moody Barber

Jennifer Butler

Jason Morris

Nico Ortiz

Tammy Goen

Isabelle Bart

Rod Goodman

Jennifer Pilates

Lisa Renee Jones

Kelly Bazzani

Kurt A. David

Chad Gaines

Misty Blakesley

Richard Steffen

Molly Milinkovich

Maryann Lombardi

Craig Wayne Boyd

Anthony F. Navarro

DEDICATION

To all those who dedicate their life to helping others live a more fulfilled life

Foreword

By Les Brown

Many of us spend at least a good part of our day going over internal dialog. We relive past experiences, worry about the future, blame the outside world for our shortcomings and criticize ourselves for not having all we want by this point in our lives. We do this both consciously and unconsciously. Even while we are listening to others, we aren't really fully present. Instead, we are rehearsing our answers, slipping back into yesterday and worrying about tomorrow.

We live in uncertain times. We all feel we have minimum control over being able to change external circumstances, but we do have control over being able to change our internal environment, not only being able to see the truth behind a given situation but also how we respond to it. And to get the best out of the most stressful times, we need to demand the best from ourselves.

Many feel the pain of unhappiness. So many suffer from it daily, unaware that they can eliminate their suffering and find happiness by simply seeing the truth behind their unhappiness and making the right choices to change it. The problem is that our emotional conflicts are so familiar to us that they keep us blinded to better possibilities. We actually become addicted to feeling the way we do, thinking that it is just the way things are and we resign ourselves to getting by and coping.

I have had the privilege of speaking for over forty years serving millions of people from over 51 different countries. I know that there are certain patterns that create success and other patterns that breed internal conflict and failures.

The secret to being fulfilled and living the life you want is having the courage to go beyond the skills you've learned and discover the gifts that you were born with and to implement them daily. So many people settle for less in life, but I can tell you from my experience that it doesn't have to be that way.

I was born in an abandoned building on a floor with a twin brother in a poor section in Miami Florida called Liberty City. When we were six weeks of age, we were adopted by Mrs. Mimi Brown. Whenever I speak, I always say that all that I am and all I ever hope to be I owe to my mother.

When I was in the fifth grade, I was labeled educable mentally retarded and put back from the fifth grade to the fourth grade and failed again when I was in the eighth grade. Mrs. Mimi Brown took my brother and I and five other kids in as foster kids and eventually adopted us.

Because of the work that Jim Britt does and the methods and techniques he uses to change your story and how you see yourself, it enabled me to build my career to make it against all odds. Both Jim Britt and Jim Lutes are icons in personal development and empowering others to be the best they can be.

You have something special inside. You have greatness in you. When you read this book it will take you on a journey and introduce you to a part of yourself that has remained hidden and you didn't know existed.

When you begin to look at your goals and dreams realize that you have greatness inside you. The Change will provide the insights and processes of self-development that will empower you to manifest your greatness.

Jim Britt and I actually started the foundation of our speaking careers in the same direct selling company, Bestline, over 40 years ago. Although I haven't followed Jim Britt's career over the years, but I do know that he is recognized as one of the top thought leaders in the world, helping millions of people create prosperous lives, rewarding relationships and spiritual awareness. He has authored 13 books and multiple programs showing people how to understand their hidden abilities to do more, become more and enjoy more in every area of life.

Today, Jim Britt and mind programming expert, Jim Lutes, along with inspiring co-authors from around the world, bring a pioneering work "The Change" book series to the market to transform lives. Their principles are forged on touching millions on every continent. As you read, you are exploring self-empowerment principles from a whole different perspective. In fact, Jim and Jim's publications of

The Change book series now has hundreds of coauthors in 26 countries. The real power in each book is that 20 coauthors share their inspiring story so that the reader may benefit from their experience. It is packed with life-changing ideas, stories, tips, strategies on various empowering topics that you will love.

The principles, concepts and ideas within this book are sometimes simple, but can be profound to a person who is ready for that perfect message at the right time and is willing to take action to change. Maybe for one it's a chapter on relationships or leadership. For the next maybe it's a chapter on forgiveness or health awareness, and for another a simple life-changing message like I received as a youngster from a teacher. Each chapter is like opening a surprise empowering gift.

As I travel the world presenting my seminars, I meet people who spend more time and energy focused on what's wrong with society and their lives than is spent on helping each other improve the quality of life. With so much time spent on social media we often fear intimate contact with each other. Mistrust is often our first reaction. We judge and sometimes brutalize those among us who are in any way different from ourselves. We become addicted to anything that allows us a brief consolidation from the terrible pain we feel inside.

We need to begin to understand more about ourselves and our condition if there is ever to be the possibility of a healthy society. I believe this is possible and that's why I am so passionate about the work I do. Simply put...we are at war with ourselves. Real healing only takes place when we are willing to experience and face the truth within.

The conclusion to me is an exciting one. You, me and every other human being are shaping our brains and bodies by the thoughts we think, the emotions we feel, the intentions we hold, and the actions we take daily. Why is it exciting? Because we are in control of all these things and we can change as long as we have the intention, willingness and commitment to look inside, take charge of our lives and make the changes.

Whether you're pursuing, your dreams as an entrepreneur, a business owner or you want a more fulfilling relationship, or simply want to live a happy life, being authentic and actively appreciating what you're really capable of is going to be one of the most important assets you possess. It will make the difference between just "getting by" and really thriving and experiencing happiness or internal conflict.

Self-knowledge provides you the emotional edge that will help you create a better life not only for yourself, but also for everyone with whom you come in contact.

This is the time to extract the best out of yourself and to use that gift to touch the lives of others.

I want to congratulate Jim Britt and Jim Lutes for making this publication series available and for allowing me to write the foreword. I honor them both and the coauthors within this book and the series for the lives they are changing.

As you enter these pages, do so slowly and with an open mind. Savor the wisdom you discover here, and then with interest and curiosity discover what rings true for you, and then take action toward the life you want.

Be prepared…because your life is about to change.

Hope to meet you one day at one of my seminars. And remember, everything you do counts!

Les Brown

Table of Contents

Foreword vii

Jim Britt 1
   Think Like Superman

Jim Lutes 13
   What You do with YOU

Anthony F. Navarro 33
   Because I Choose to

Misty Blakesley 43
   My Journey to Becoming

Nicole Ortiz 53
   Love is a Funny Thing

Craig Wayne Boyd 63
   I'm Still Here

Anoush Khaze 73
   Nurture Your Mind to Cultivate Success

Jennifer Pilates 83
   How to Live an Empowered Life from Within

Rich Steffen 93
   Creating A Successful Personal Structure

Stacie Barber 103
   Taking the Leap - Leaning into Truth

Rod Goodman 111
   Halfway to Cancun!

Isabelle Bart 119
  Be The Boss of Your Life
Kurt A. David 127
  Leading Change
Maryann Lombardi 135
  The Power of Knowing What you Want
Jason Morris 143
  The Power to Summon: Reclaiming Your Strength Through Directional Harmony
Jennifer Butler 153
  Broken Wide Open
Kelly Bazzani 163
  Resilience in Recovery: Phoenix Risen
Lisa Renee Jones 173
  Stay At Home Mom to Six Figures
Molly Milinkovich 183
  Moments
Chad Gaines 191
  The Chad Gaines Story
Jonathan Amundsen 199
  Change as Empirical Science
Tammy Goen 209
  Surviving to Thriving: Self Love and the Highly Sensitive Person
Afterword 219

Jim Britt

Jim Britt is an award-winning author of 15 best-selling books and nine #1 International best-sellers. Some of his many titles include Rings of Truth, Do This. Get Rich-For Entrepreneurs, Unleashing Your Authentic Power, The Power of Letting Go, Cracking the Rich Code and The Entrepreneur.

He is an internationally recognized business and life strategist who is highly sought after as a keynote speaker, both online and live, for all audiences.

As an entrepreneur Jim has launched 28 successful business ventures. He has served as a success strategist to over 300 corporations worldwide and was recently named as one of the world's top 50 speakers and top 20 success coaches. He was presented with the "Best of the Best" award out of the top 100 contributors of all time to the Direct Selling industry.

For over four decades Jim has presented seminars throughout the world sharing his success strategies and life enhancing realizations with over 5,000 audiences, totaling almost 2,000,000 people from all walks of life.

Early in his speaking career he was Business partners with the late Jim Rohn for eight years, where Tony Robbins worked under Jim's direction for his first few years in the speaking business.

As a performance strategist, Jim leverages his skills and experience as one of the leading experts in peak performance, entrepreneurship and personal empowerment to produce stellar results. He is pleased to work with small business entrepreneurs, and anyone seeking to remove the blocks that stop their success in any area of their life.

One of Jim's latest programs "Cracking the Rich Code" focuses on the subconscious programs influencing one's relationship with money and their financial success.

www.CrackingTheRichCode.com

Think Like Superman

By Jim Britt

"Waking up to your true greatness in life requires letting go of who you imagine yourself to be."

--- Jim Britt

FACT: Becoming a millionaire is easier than it has ever been.

Many people have the notion that it's an impossible task to become a millionaire. Some say, "It's pure luck." Others say, "You have to be born into a rich family." For others, "You'll have to win the Lotto." And for many they say, "Your parents have to help you out a lot." That's the language of the poor.

A single mother with five children says, "I want to believe in what you're saying. However, I'm 45 years old and work long hours at two dead-end jobs. I barely earn enough to get by. What should I do?"

Another man said, "Well, if you work for the government, you cannot expect to become a millionaire. After all, you're on a fixed salary and there's little time for anything else. By the time you get home, you've got to play with the kids, eat dinner, and fall asleep watching TV."

Everyone has a story as to why they could never become a millionaire. But for every story, excuse really, there are other stories OR PEOPLE with worse circumstances, that have become rich.

The truth is that all of us can become as wealthy as we decide to be, and that's a mindset. None of us is excluded from wealth. If you have the desire to receive money, whatever the amount, you have all of the rights to do so like everyone else. There is no limit to how much you can earn for yourself. The only limitations are what you place on yourself.

Money is like the sun. It does not discriminate. It doesn't say, "I will not give light and warmth to this flower, tree, or person because I don't like them." Like the sun, money is abundantly available to all of us who truly believe that it is for us. No one is excluded.

There are, however, some major differences between rich and poor people. Here are some tips for becoming rich.

Change Your Thinking

You have to see the bigger picture. There are opportunities everywhere! The problem is that most people see just trees, when they should be looking at the entire forest. By doing so you will see that there are opportunities everywhere. The possibilities are endless.

You'll also have to go through plenty of <u>self-discovery</u> before you earn your first million. Knowing the truth about yourself isn't always the easiest task. Sometimes, you'll find that you are your biggest enemy—at least some days.

Learn from Millionaires

Most people are surrounded by what I like to call their, "default friends." These friends are acquaintances that we see at the gym, school, work, local happy hour, and other places. We naturally befriend these people because we are all in the same boat financially. However, in most cases, these people aren't millionaires and cannot help you become one either. In fact, if you tell them you are going to become a millionaire, some may even tell you that it's impossible and discourage you from even trying. They'll tell you that you're living in a fantasy world and why you'll never be able to make it happen. Instead, learn from millionaires. Let go of these relationships that pull you down when it comes to your money desires. It's okay to have friends that aren't millionaires. However, only take input from those that have accomplished what you want to accomplish. Hang out with those that will encourage and help you get to the next level. Don't give your raw diamonds to a brick layer to be cut.

Indulge in Wealth

To become wealthy, you must learn about wealth. This means that you'll have to put yourself in situations that you've never been in before.

ON OCCASION, DO SOME OF THESE:

Fly first class and see how it makes you feel.

Eat out at the finest restaurant and don't look at the price.

Take a limo instead of a cab or Uber. Watch how you feel.

Reserve a suite in a first-class hotel.

If you are used to drinking a $20 bottle of wine, go for the $100 and see how it tastes. It does taste different.

All I am saying is, try some of the things that wealthy people do and see how it makes you feel.

Believe it is Possible

If you believe that it is possible to become a millionaire, you can make it happen. However, if you've excluded yourself from this possibility and think and believe that it's for other people, you'll never become a millionaire.

Also, be sure to bless rich people when you can. Haters of money aren't likely to receive any of it either.

Read books that have been written by millionaires. By gaining a well-rounded education about earning large sums of money and staying inspired, you'll be able to learn the wealth secrets of the rich. I just saw a video on LinkedIn with my friend Kevin Harrington from the TV show Shark Tank. He said that one of his new companies just had a million-dollar day on Amazon.

Enlarge Your Service

Your material wealth is the sum of your total contribution to society. Your daily mantra should be, *'How do I deliver more value to more people in less time?'* Then, you'll know that you can always increase your quality and quantity of service. Enlarging your service is also about going the extra mile. When it comes to helping others, you must give it everything you have. You just plant the seeds and nature will take care of the rest.

Seize ALL Opportunities That Make Sense

You cannot say "No" to opportunities and expect to become a millionaire. You must seize every opportunity that has your name on it. It may just be an opportunity to connect with an influential person for no reason. Sometimes the monetary reward will not come immediately, but if you keep planting seeds, eventually you'll grow a fruitful crop. Money is the harvest of the service you provide and sometimes the connections you have. The more seeds you plant, the greater the harvest.

Have an Unstoppable Mindset

Want to know some of what my first mentor shared with me that took me from a broke factory worker, high school dropout, to millionaire?

First, he said, you have to start thinking like a wealthy, unstoppable person. You have to have a wealth mindset. He said that wealthy people think differently. He said, "I want you to start thinking like Superman!" Sounds crazy, right? Well, it's not. It's powerful and here's why. How you think will change your life.

Wealthy people think differently. They really do. And anyone can learn to think like the wealthy.

I'm not talking about positive thinking, Law of Attraction, or motivation. Let's get real. None of that stuff works anyway. Otherwise, we would all be rich and happy already. I'm talking about thinking based in quantum physics science. Once you understand and apply it, it will change your life. You will become unstoppable!

If there was any person, fictional or real, whose qualities you could instantly possess, who would that person be? Think about it. Personally, I would say that Superman is the perfect person. Now, you are probably thinking I have lost it right? Just stick with me here. I think you will like what you are about to hear.

Superman is a fictional superhero widely considered to be one of the most famous and popular action hero and an American cultural icon. I remember watching Superman every Saturday morning when I was a kid. I couldn't get enough. He was my hero!

Let's look at Superman's traits:

Superman is indestructible.

He is a man of steel.

He can stop a locomotive in its tracks.

Bullets bounce off him.

He is faster than a speeding bullet.

No one can bring him down.

He can leap tall buildings in a single bound. Great powers to have in this day-and-age, wouldn't you say? What else would you need?

Now, for all you females, don't worry, we have not left you out. There is also a female version of Superman, named Superwoman. She has the same powers as Superman.

Now, this is where it gets interesting. Let's first look at the qualities that Superman possesses that you want to make your own. And to make it simple, I will refer to Superman for the rest of this message, and you can replace with Superwoman if you are female.

Again:

Superman is powerful and fearless.

Superman is virtually indestructible—except for kryptonite of course.

Superman can stop bullets.

Superman has supernatural powers. He can see through walls.

Superman can stop a speeding locomotive.

Superman can stop a bullet.

Superman jumps into immediate action when troubles arise.

Superman can crash through barriers.

Superman can even change clothes in a phone booth in seconds. Not too many of those around anymore. You'll have to duck behind a building to change.

So, you're thinking right now, *'Ok, I know that Superman has incredible supernatural powers, how can that help me? What good will it do me to think I am Superman, a fictional character?'*

Here is where science comes in. This is the part where you will be amazed when you learn about the supernatural powers that you already possess! NO, REALLY!

Your brain makes certain chemicals called neuro peptides. These are literally the molecules of emotion, like love, fear, joy, passion, and so on. These molecules of emotion are not only contained in your brain they actually circulate throughout your cellular structure. They send out a signal, a frequency much like a radio station sending out a signal. For example, you tune to 92.5 and you get jazz. Tune to 99.6 and you get rock. And if you are just one decimal off, you get static. The difference is that your signal goes both ways. You are a sender and a receiver.

You put out a signal, a mindset, of confidence about your financial success and people, circumstances, and opportunities show up to support your success. When you put out a signal of doubt and uncertainty and you receive support for your doubt and uncertainty. You've been around someone that you didn't trust, or you felt less than positive just being in their presence, right? You have also been around people that inspire you. That's what I'm talking about. You are projecting a frequency, looking to resonate with the frequency you are transmitting.

Anyway, the amazing part about these cells of emotion is that they are intelligent. They are thinking cells. These cells are constantly eavesdropping on the conversation that you are having with yourself. That's right. They are listening to you! And others are listening to your cells as well. Others feel what you feel when they are around you.

Your unconscious mind, your cells, are listening in, waiting to adjust your behavior based on what they hear from you, their master. So just imagine what would happen if you started to think like Superman...or like a millionaire.

Here are some of the thoughts you might have during the day:

"The challenges I face day today are easily overcome, after all I am Superman."

"I am indestructible."

"I have incredible strength."

"Nothing can stop me.....NOTHING."

"I have supernatural powers and can overcome anything."

"I can accomplish anything I want when I put my mind to it."

"I can break through any barrier."

"I can and I will do whatever it takes to accomplish my goal."

"I fear nothing."

The trillions of thinking cells in your body and brain listen, and they create exactly what you tell them to create. Their mission is to complete the picture of the you they see and hear when you talk to them. They must obey. It's their job!

Since you are Superman, you cannot fail. Why? Your thinking cells are now sending out the right signal, because you told them to. They are making you stronger, more successful, everyday! You have the ability to fight off all negativity, doubt, fear, and worry—nothing can stop you!

Superman has total confidence. So, your cells of emotion relating to confidence will now create more neuro peptide chemicals to promote feelings of power and confidence that others will feel in your presence.

Superman is fearless. So, your cells of emotion relating to fear will now create more neuro peptide chemicals to create feelings of courage. You are unstoppable!

And here's the key. Others will respond to you in the same way that you are talking to yourself.

If you are confident, others will have confidence in you.

You have thousands of thoughts every day. Make sure your thoughts are leading you in the direction you want to go. Make sure you are telling your cells a success story, and not a 'woe is me' story.

Most have been conditioned to think that creating wealth is difficult, or that it's only for the lucky few. What do you believe? It doesn't cost you any more to think like Superman; and it's much more inspiring!

Mediocrity cannot be an option if you decide to be wealthy and think like Superman.

Your decision, and communication with your cells, creates a mindset; that mindset influences how you show up.

None of that old type of thinking matters anymore…after all, you are Superman, and you can accomplish anything.

If you want wealth, you have to stretch yourself. You have to do the things that unsuccessful people are not willing to do. You have to say "yes" to opportunity, then figure out how to get the job done.

Maybe you are uncomfortable selling and asking for money. If that's the case, then learn sales and learn to ask for money every day until you feel comfortable asking for it. You will never have money if you don't learn to ask for it.

I've learned a lot in the past 40+ years as an entrepreneur. I've learned that in order to have more, you have to become more. I've also learned that if you are comfortable, you are not growing. I learned that I couldn't go from a nervous rookie speaker with minimal self-confidence to hosting TV shows and speaking in front of 5,000 people overnight. I simply wasn't ready. I grew into that, one speaking engagement at a time. Every time I finished a speaking engagement, I would ask myself, "How did I do, and how could I do it better?" I still do that today.

And I've learned from the hundreds of thousands of people I've trained, coached, and mentored that none of us can do something we don't believe is possible. It's not going to happen if you're not ready to step out of your comfort zone and stretch yourself.

This has led me to understand the single most important principle of wealth-building, that has meant the difference between poverty and riches for people since humans first traded for pelts.

Are you ready?

Come in just a little closer. Listen up!

Every income level requires a different you, a different mindset! If you think that $10,000 a month is a lot of money, then $100,000 a month will be completely out of reach. If you believe that having $5,000 in the bank would make you rich, then $50,000 won't miraculously appear. You will never earn more money than you believe is "a lot" of money.

What you do as a business is only a small part of becoming rich. In fact, there are thousands, if not tens of thousands, of ways to make money—and lots of it. What I've learned over the years is that, by focusing on who you want to become instead of what you need to do, you're going to multiply your chances of getting rich a hundred-fold.

Ask anyone who's found a way to make a large sum of money legally, and he or she will tell you that it's not hard once you crack the code. And cracking the code starts with you and your mindset. The "code" to which I refer isn't a secret rite or ancient scroll. It's not even a secret. It's a certain way of thinking and believing in which you've trained your mind to see money-making ideas.

That's where you see a need in the marketplace, and you jump on the idea quickly. It might involve creating a new product; or, it may just be teaching others a special technique you've learned. It may even require raising capital to start a company or to market a product or idea on social media.

Don't Hold Back. You Have to Take Action to Change.

Start right now to imagine yourself as already having wealth. How would your life be? How would your day unfold? Start to own your wealth mindset now! The subconscious mind is unable to differentiate between actual fact and mere visualization. So, by imagining that you already have it, you're encouraging your subconscious mind to seek the ways and means to transform your imaginary feelings into the real thing.

Find yourself some mentors. Nobody has all the answers. Surround yourself with people that will support, inspire, and provide you with answers that keep you moving in the right direction. If you truly want to attain wealth, have a thriving business, or reach the top of your game in any endeavor, having a qualified mentor is essential.

Okay, lets come in for a landing ...

It is absolutely essential to have a crystal-clear picture of what you want to accomplish before you begin. If you want to attain wealth, you must learn to operate without fear and with a sharply defined mental image of the outcome you want to attain. This comes from thinking like a wealthy person, (like Superman) making decisions like a wealthy person and being fearless (like Superman) when it comes to stepping out of your comfort zone. Look at the end result as something you're already prepared to do, you just haven't done it yet.

Think about this. Your success is something that you have been preventing; it's not something you have to struggle to make happen. The key is to not let fear, doubt, other people, or mind chatter push your success away. You'll find that the solutions taking you toward your goals will come to you in the most unexpected and sudden ways. You don't need the *perfect* plan first. What you need is a perfectly clear decision about your success, the right mindset, the right mentoring, and the ideal way to get you there will materialize.

The greatest transfer of wealth in the history of the human race is happening right now. Are you positioned to get your share?

Remember, in order to get a different result, you must do something different. In order to do something different you must know something different to do. And in order to know something different, you have to first suspect that your present methods need improving.

THEN, YOU HAVE TO BE WILLING TO DO SOMETHING ABOUT IT.

***

For more information on Jim's work:

www.JimBritt.com

http://JimBrittCoaching.com

www.facebook.com/jimbrittonline

www.linkedin.com/in/jim-britt

For free audio series www.RichCode1.com and www.RichCode2.com

http://becomeAcoauthor.com

To find out how to crack the rich code and change your subconscious programming regarding your relationship with money: www.CrackingTheRichCode.com

Jim Lutes

Say the name Jim Lutes and chances are a top performer in your company has attended one or more of his dynamic trainings over the last few years.

Having taught his branded form of human performance since the early 1990s, Mr. Lutes has accelerated top level entrepreneurs throughout his career by conducting trainings on personal growth and subconscious programming into worldwide markets.

During this time Jim took his skills regarding the human mind, and combining it with trainings on influence, persuasion and communication strategies he launched Lutes International in the early 1990s. Based in San Diego California Jim has taught seminars for, corporations, sales forces, individuals and athletes. Having appeared on television, radio and worldwide stages, Jim's style, knowledge and effectiveness provide profound results.

"Jim Lutes possesses a unique ability to create performance change in an individual in a fraction of the time it takes his competitors". The core of human's decisions is based on the programs we acquire, reinforce and grow. Combining Jims various trainings individuals can reach new levels of achievement and fulfillment in all areas of life. The results are at times nothing short of astonishing.

"My goal is to take that embryonic greatness that exists inside every person in America, foster it, empower it and then hand them personal strategies based on solid principles that allow them to take that new attitude and apply it to creating a life masterpiece".

What You do with YOU

By Jim Lutes

Most people think that if they can just learn enough, earn enough, get smart enough, then they will BE enough. And they think that when that happens, they can finally relax and be happy. But what happens is that they get so caught up in what they are constantly *doing* that are not focused on how they are *being*.

In other words, they are not focused on their emotional state. When you engage your emotions you subconscious mind begins to get the messages and begins to establish new rules and new behaviors. And then it becomes a way of life and enters your heart and really begins to come from your heart. When it is in your heart then it is truly part of you. When you are really getting it now at the deepest level, when you can begin to anticipate what I am going to say, you know you understand it at a much deeper level right now.

I began to study human performance as a way to make some changes in my own life and when I began to see some serious results, I got so excited about it that I wanted to share it with other people. And so I committed my life to learning and sharing what works with others. So, I am a committed lifetime learner and therefore I have been fortunate enough to have had the ability to look at and study just about every approach there is to personal development and success that is available in today's market. I am a strong advocate of clear, simple, workable approaches that get dependable and lasting results.

Because of the vast wealth of information my Life Masterpiece teaching gives you and the amazing results you will get, you will likely find yourself returning to it again and again throughout your life.

No matter how successful we are, or how successful we become, we all need a coach to encourage us, to challenge us, to remind us to live up to our potential. I am going to be here to do that for you each day, and it is both my honor and my privilege to serve you in that way.

Let's get started now.

That person that you are and that person that you must become in order to put the colors of your life masterpiece where you want them and blend them in just the right combination to create your own unique experience might right now seem like two very different people, but they are one in the same. You are that person right now. I am going to help you uncover your true identity and purpose so that you can then activate the universal laws and make them work for you.

When we let go of all the stories, we have been telling ourselves about who we think we are supposed to be and what we think we are supposed to do and have, we not only free ourselves we free our families, our children, our intimate partners, and our friends in the process. There is no way you can make a difference in yourself without touching somebody else even if it is not your intention.

The Life Masterpiece focus is about what you can do with YOU. If you want to change any circumstance, any relationship, then you must begin with yourself no matter how convinced you are that somebody else or something else must change. Changing yourself can change even the most rigid system and stubborn person. And ANY progress moves you forward. And any movement forward on your part creates the opportunity for every other part of your life to be moved forward as well.

One of the most effective ways for you to reprogram your mind is through what I like to call vicarious experiences. These are the experiences other people have had and I will bring you through their experiences by sharing their stories with you. These stories are not in this book simply to fill it up and make it fat like you find in some books. These stories are the heart and soul of the book because this is how you will begin to reprogram your subconscious and take the information into your heart where it will transform you.

The reason why vicarious experiences are so powerful is because they relate to you and so when you are reading these stories your conscious mind will get go and your unconscious mind will get the lesson.

And when you read some of these remarkable stories and meet some of these people who have gone through some amazing personal transformations, you will begin to realize that no matter who you are, no matter what part of the world you are from or what culture you grew up in, whether you grow up poor, wealthy or somewhere in between, whether you grow up with religion or Monday Night Football, you will begin to realize that we all have the same problems.

So what will happen is you will begin to connect with these people because they have the same problems you have- the same challenges. They are universal. And you will learn what the reason is for this is that we all have the same basic needs, and our lives are about meeting these needs and that they impact and determine every single thing we do and every decision we make. Every single habit, behavior, rule or pattern is your unconscious way of trying to get your needs met. And your needs are the same exact needs every other human being on the planet has. We all use different behaviors to get these needs met but they are still the same.

Some of the behaviors we use are positive and healthy and some of them are not quite so resourceful. And this is one of the reasons why even though we all have the same needs and the same problems, we all get different results. We are hard wired with the same needs, but not with the same subconscious programming. And the reason why we all get different results boils down to one thing- standards.

You know, so often in life, we find ourselves in a position where we live life a certain way. We act a certain way. We were raised a certain way. And through our lives in an effort to avoid pain and still meet our needs, we made critical decisions about who we are and how we think we need to be. And so we believe we know who we are.

But the way we have behaved for years is simply an *adaptation*. Something that happened in response to the desire we had to meet our basic needs- to get the love, or respect, or acceptance from a parent, lover, loved one or peers- caused us to make a key decision and adapt to the circumstances around us. We do not ever realize that for years we have been living something that we are really good at but which is not necessarily our true nature.

One of the things you will learn here is that a single decision has the power to change everything in a heartbeat. In fact, when you stay with me through this you are going to learn about a decision, he made perhaps some time ago that his determine the choices you have made in the course of your life up until now. Today he made a decision to pick up this book and begin this journey with me and if you will indulge me for just a few hours the decision to pick up this book might be the decision that changes everything in your life from today on.

Now that you've made the decision to read it, I will tell you what this book can really do for you. It will get you to uncover and maybe for the first time really identify how the role models of your life have affected your subconscious decision-making in ways you never dreamed possible.

Without getting into the actual science behind it, a child's brain works much differently than an adult brain. As you might already know our brains operate using four different wavelengths -- alpha, beta, theta and Delta. Most of the time, the adult brain operates at the beta level when we are awake. The beta level is when our eyes are focused in our conscious mind is in control, and we are logical. The alpha level is a level that we must pass through to go to sleep and to wake up, and it's also the most common level is one we are in a trance. Theta is for a deeper trance or dreaming, and Delta is for deep sleep. This means that when we are at the alpha level, we are highly impressionable, because the messages are going directly into our subconscious minds. A child's mind is different because it operates primarily at the alpha level, which is why children are so impressionable. This also means that our parents and other significant people in our childhood had a tremendous impact on the messages that are subconscious mind received and events from our childhood had a strong impact on our self-image, our identity and how we develop as adults. This is why when we speak about reprogramming the subconscious mind is very important to talk about her childhood and her relationship with her parents. This is not done to point fingers or place blame, but to help us understand some of the reasons for the choices that we make for the patterns that we keep repeating and how they carry over from generation to generation.

Even if you feel like you held your own when you were growing up, and that the relationships that you had as a child -- especially the relationship she had with your mother and father -- were strong, and you feel like you are strong as a result. There are still patterns that your subconscious mind is running that no longer serve you. Because it's the tension, the experience of having to deal with all of the events of your past and even the events that happened before you were born in your parent's past -- all of these experiences affect your decision making, your relationships, your finances, your choices, behaviors and life circumstances, even today.

Even if your childhood was perfect and you feel like you honor, respect and love your parents and adore all of your siblings and even if your parents or your greatest role models, you are still affected on many levels and in many ways. And because you decided to read this book, I believe you have some things you would like to change. If you change anything, first you must learn to reprogram your subconscious mind and part of doing so is to understand that the key decisions you made in the past still impact you today.

Our childhood role models deeply affect both our conscious and are subconscious decision-making and behavior patterns. We are all examples, and some of us are warnings. We all, at one time or another, impact other people. This is one of the reasons why I stress that it is so important to live consciously and be an example.

When I ask people about their belief systems and the habits and patterns that basically control their lives, I am often struck by how few of these beliefs and habits were ever chosen by that person on a conscious level. In other words, the rules that are guiding your life about how to BE in your own life very often picked up unconsciously.

It is incredible how common it is that people start this process, and when they begin to reassess their lives and their relationships with themselves and others in the success they are having or perhaps not having, they discover that much of what has been screwing up their lives, their achievements, their finances, their careers, their intimate relationships, and even their bodies (and I am not talking about the excuse many of us use about genetics. Being the reason, our bodies look the way they do) was influenced by their PARENTS. Not by their parents' problems necessarily, but by somehow trying to be liked, loved or appreciated by one parent. Many times, these decisions also have to do with trying to avoid pain that was inflicted by a parent or other significant role model, or simply standing up to a parent.

We can be 4050. Even 80 years old, and we are still living the strategies of a child.

And what's even worse, is it very often when we were a kid, we said, "I'll never be like that!" And here you are today, exactly like that! You don't want to admit it but if you held up a mirror and watched a film of your interactions you would say, "Oh my God, I never wanted to be like that parent." And yet you are. Or perhaps you have done the opposite. Perhaps you have thrown the pendulum the other way and you're not like that parent at all. Now, you are something worse. Or, let's just say you are something else. You are the opposite of the extreme you didn't like. And so now you are another extreme, that doesn't work either. Because no one teaches us this stuff, and so it becomes unconscious. We don't even see it. It's part of the invisible fabric of our thinking and our decision-making every single day.

This book will give you a unique opportunity to look deep inside yourself. It will allow you to look inside of your relationships, your decisions about money, and your decisions about your career, your relationship with God or your higher power, and even your body. It will allow you to understand how your own up bringing us may be influenced you and you probably know a lot of the ways it has influenced you, but maybe you'll spot some of the decisions you have made, maybe even one core decision that has affected your identity.

So, what the heck does identity mean anyway? It can be such a big and often loaded word. Well, I believe identity is the strongest force in the human personality. If you want to know what shapes you the most it's not your capability. It's your identity and the rules you have for who you think you are.

And you know what the challenge is? Most of us to defined ourselves a long time ago. And when we step outside that definition, we get really uncomfortable, because the strongest force in the human personality is the need to remain consistent with how we define ourselves. Later, we will talk about the human needs are referred to earlier. One of them is certainty. What this means is that if certainty is one of the deepest needs we have, then if you don't know who you are, you do not know how to act.

Very early in life, we begin to define who we are. We use labels such as loner, aggressive conservative, sexy, successful loser rich poor in charge. I work for others. I am ugly. I am smart. I am a procrastinator. I am clumsy. I am athletic. I am thin. I am big boned. What happens is these definitions become self-fulfilling prophecies, because nobody wants to be disappointed. Nobody wants to live in a place of uncertainty. So, there may be arranging your identity or in your definition of yourself, but it may not be absolute.

The metaphor that you so often hear of what we talk about our comfort zone, is that our comfort zone is like a thermostat. We all have our comfort zone, and it is set by our subconscious mind. So, if your subconscious mind has set your thermostat a particular area of your life, for example how much money you make, that let's say 45°, and if the temperature drops down to 40°, guess what happens? It doesn't meet your identity. In other words, things are not good enough, whether it be mentally and emotionally financially with your weight (which by the way is the primary reason people whose weight tend to gain it back because they lose it before reprogramming their subconscious mind to reset the thermostat) or whatever.

For example, if you drop down to 40° and your finances and 45° is your identity. This means that 45° is what you must have. Or, if you drop down to 70° in your intimacy and 80° is your identity, then this is what you must have. Whatever it is, when you drop below your comfort zone, you will be compelled to drive to make it better automatically. If your body gets out of control, there is a point at which you go, "that's enough!" You are willing to be a little off your identity but not that much. And suddenly you go on the diet suddenly make the change because you feel the pressure that comes with being inconsistent with your own definition of how you think you should be.

But what most of us fail to recognize is that this happens on the other side as well. Your subconscious mind since your mental thermostat at say 45° for your finances or 80° mentally for how close you want to be with your intimate partner, or 70° for how your body should look and feel,

This is not your *goal*. Your goal is something much larger. This is your subconscious comfort zone or your subconscious definition of yourself. For example, you might think of yourself as big boned, but if it suddenly isn't good enough and you really become overweight, then you change to fit your self-image or your definition of yourself in order to get back into that comfort zone. But also, if it gets better than you expected, perhaps, you lose a lot of weight and get really good shape, or perhaps you lead your company in sales for two quarters in a row when you normally come in third or fourth, or perhaps you jump from 70° in your intimacy, and now you have a relationship that is at 90 or even 100°. You have a really hot, passionate relationship with more passion than you ever have before, or you lose three dress sizes instead of one, or you double your income, whatever it is, your subconscious mind starts talking some sense into you. And your brain goes, "Hello, dude what the heck are you doing? You are 70 degree-er, what in heck are you doing way appear at 90? You can't keep that. That's not gonna last. Get back down to 70° before you get hurt or fail or screw it up. You're in over your head. You're not an entrepreneur. You work for other people."

Wherever your subconscious mind has set your comfort zone based on the way you define yourself, you're going to keep adjusting to stay in that comfort zone. So many times, in these types of programs, people challenge you to get out of your comfort zone, which you can't do consciously. You have to go into your subconscious and reset your comfort zone, just like you would the thermostat. And this will keep happening until you reprogram your subconscious mind with a new identity, and the new comfort zone. Before you set out to make any kind of lasting change, you must reset your subconscious comfort zone.

And what do we do when we exceed our comfort zone? Well, what happened is that the drive to make things better stops. And so you stop growing and gradually you drift back until you reach your comfort zone. Or worse, you start to sabotage. The mental air conditioners kick on bring yourself right back down to where you think you deserve to be based on your subconscious identity.

For example, if the only kind of love you view as a child was abuse, the only kind of life. You knew was living paycheck to paycheck or in debt, or the only kind of lifestyle you ever experienced with sedentary, whatever it is, even though it might be painful. It is what you know. This becomes your comfort zone and therefore provides the certainty that you need. It becomes your self-definition and what you think you deserve. You begin to think -- not consciously, but unconsciously -- this IS love, this is just the body. You inherited, or that wealth is for other kind of people, or you're not the right kind of person to make certain kinds of social contacts. Of course, this is not your conscious thinking that this is what is going on in your subconscious. That is why we often don't get the results we are after, or continue to sabotage the matter, what types of technology, techniques and information we add to our bag of tricks.

And therein lays the trouble, or perhaps a better way to say it, the shortcomings with many of the programs you may have tried in the past. They pump you up and felt good about it. They motivated you with affirmations and taught you use visualization. They've even taught you that the universal laws work for everyone. You may have even made some changes, but they did not last. Because when you're taught these things, you know the stuff in your head on a conscious level. But your identity and self-definition is the thermostat of subconscious mind, so before you can make any substantive or lasting change, first you must reprogram your subconscious mind and change who you are at the deepest level. (Green papers).

In other words, you must become the kind of person who has whatever it is that you want. Visualizing it, affirming it, and even living your life by a new set of standards is not going to work long term until this stuff goes from your conscious to your unconscious and finally into your heart. Not only do you have to DO it, and not only do you have to LIVE it, but you also have to BECOME it. And then you will manifest it.

And that is the difference between the stick figure you are drawing now or the paint by numbers life you have been taught to lead and the masterpiece you are now creating. So for the colors in our masterpiece is to really live consciously, to be an example, then we have to get conscious about what is shaping us and the thing that shapes you most identity.

Someone who is outrageous will behave, say things differently and move differently than someone who believes they are extremely conservative. They will use a different voice, a different way of moving and different language. Here is my question for you:

When did you come up with this definition?

When did you decide that is who you are?

When was the last time you updated it?

Maybe it's time to take another look at who you are today. And maybe you don't have to actually give up your identity. Maybe the identity of created for yourself is magnificent, but maybe it's time to expand it. Maybe it's time to add to it. Maybe it's time to open up to a new level of freedom and options.

And when you do that there will be a processional effect in all areas of your life, because we are all connected in a cybernetic loop. If I want to change you, I can try to control you, but that will not change anything. Or I can try to change the system, but that will not last or will be futile. Or, I can change me into an ID that everything changes.

For example, if I change the way I treat you the way I respond to you my voice my body my feelings and my emotions by respect for you. It will affect the way you feel and the way you respond back. And the same is true with the universe and higher intelligence. Once you change yourself, reprogram your subconscious, become the person you need to become that the things that you want in your life, then you will begin to receive a different response from the universe in a different result in your life. Then begin to experience your life as a masterpiece.

You will learn that what we value controls what we are willing to do or not do -- in our businesses, and our relationships, with our bodies and with her children. Some people get locked in place into a mindset. I call it being committed to your commitment. For example, have you ever been in an argument, and you were so angry that as the argument progressed, you forgot what you were angry about, and it just became about winning? We've all been there and what happens is we get committed to being angry and said that resolving the argument. Or we get committed to being right, instead of uncovering the truth. When this happens, get so wrapped up in our commitment that we can no longer see the forest through the trees. We lose touch with what we really want, because we get stuck in a mindset, and we get committed to our commitments.

(Judy- discovers a decision she made as a child and uses the discovery to transform her life and her children and grandchildren's lives).

Today, you are beginning a process that can truly change the quality of your life forever and can take that paint by numbers life you might be living now and create the masterpiece called your life. So just for a moment now, what I want you to do is imagine that your life is a painting. And imagine that you have died and are looking down at that painting. What did you leave behind? Is your life, a masterpiece that is cherished and hangs prominently as an example for others of what is possible, or is it a paint-by-numbers life that is packed away in someone's basement?

As you begin this process, I asked for only two things from you:

1. Your heartfelt desire to make real changes.
2. The commitment to follow through and do this, as simple or as located as it might seem in the moment.

If you can do just those two things, then the things that you used to call dreams will become part of your daily reality.

Why is it that you can have a person who seems to have superior abilities, talents, skills, and education, the same time, they don't produce the quality of life they want or that you might expect from them? And why is it, on the other hand, you can have someone who seemingly has every disadvantage -- no family support, the wrong social status, no emotional support, no education, and the wrong background -- and yet they go out and produce results, way beyond what anyone could have expected or even imagined?

The difference in our quality of life is not about our capability, background or education. Human beings, *that means you*, are *all capable* of achieving incredible results, and yet sadly only a few seem to get it.

What people WILL do is very different from what people CAN do.

I want to challenge you right now to start using your WILL muscle, instead of your TRY muscle, which is probably overdeveloped anyhow. I challenge you to start exercising your inborn human power, which is your birthright as a member of the human race, your ability to act based on the choice and free will that every human has in equal measure. Frankly, this means that if it has been achieved, then there is no reason on earth why you cannot achieve it. And beyond that, if it can be imagined, then there is also very little reason why you cannot achieve it. As a matter of fact, your unconscious mind will rarely imagine something that you are capable of. That is the difference between desires and fantasies. It's true. There are no excuses anymore. If you are reading this and you are human being that you have the ability to take action and to produce results.

Disability that I'm talking about is not something I can give you. Why? Because you already have it. You were born, great. Now, I challenge you to go out and take back what is rightfully yours.

Hopefully, something is now a weekend within you in two ways. One, by igniting your desire and two by showing you some simple systematic strategies on how you can get greater results out of yourself on a daily basis.

When most of us think of success or failure, we tend to think of these monumental things. Failure is not an overnight thing, and neither is success.

Just what is success? Well, some people describe it in terms of achievements like our resume. But it is different for everyone. So some people describe it as a feeling. It's your difficult for you to make it a goal to achieve a feeling for something that is difficult to define. Many programs attempt to do that, and they use motivation to give you that temporary feeling of success. But it doesn't last.

The truth is that success is actually wrapped up in failure. What I mean by that is that success is simply a string of failures all going in the same purposeful direction. That's right. If you want to find success you have to look inside a failure. In other words, if you want to be more successful than the next person, then you simply have to be willing to experience more failure, but not just any failures. You must be willing to take specific actions, based on specific decisions, fail most of the time, keep going, perhaps with a new strategy, experience and more failures, and eventually you will succeed. If this sounds painful, then I want you to think for a moment about what true failure actually is.

True failure is lifelong failure. It is the failure of inactivity. It's not actually failing at what you DO -- those things will lead to success. But when you fail to DO, you fail to succeed. In failing to do is a recipe for ultimate failure in life. When you fail to make the calls, when you fail to follow through, when you fail to say I love you, when you fail to give your all, that is what creates the ultimate failure in life. Ultimate failure creates the greatest pain, the feelings we want to avoid at all costs. Now *that* is painful.

Success happens one step at a time. Actually, success happens one failure at a time. It is successfully making the calls and doing it no matter how long it takes for the outcome in the moment. It is successfully getting up and following through. It is successfully making sure that you make that unique contact. It is successfully breaking through the limits that used to stop you.

Success is a combination of all those little things -- those little successes that often come disguised as failures -- over each day and over your lifetime that eventually create a life that you will have total pride and great joy in knowing that you created your life and made it into a masterpiece of your very own -- a life that is an example to others as how it is done.

The purpose of Life Masterpiece is to show you how to tap the power you were born with and how to tap into it every single day. And to make it an effortless process so that it becomes a lifestyle.

Before I go any further, I want to thank you for your friendship. Even though I have never met you, personally, I feel as if you and I are kindred spirits. The reason why say that is it you picked up this book. You made an investment. You're now reading it. This means you are one of the few who will do what others will not. This puts you light years ahead of 99% of the people. You and I encounter every day. Those people are living a paint-by-numbers life. They want to change, but they just do not get it, because they haven't got the first clue what they want and worse, they are not willing to do anything to change it.

I know you're special because you are researching and exploring and because you are reading this. It says something to me about you. It tells me that you are willing to do what it takes to succeed. It tells me that you are not satisfied with your life, and you will not be satisfied until you have successfully created your own masterpiece. So, I really want to give you the tools that can make a difference.

I have dedicated my life to understanding what makes people do what they do. What drives you? What is it that makes the difference in performance from one human being to the next? If we are all born with the same stuff, what causes some to tap into it and others to settle for a mediocre, paint-by-numbers existence?

Power comes from concentrating your focus and taking daily action to improve something. Even a 1% improvement today can result in unbelievable change, because 1% per day will not give you a 365% difference in being the year, because it builds and compounds to create a difference, way beyond anything you can probably imagine right now.

I will show you how to make it happen quickly, not 10 or 20 years from now, but today. Anything you commit to and focus on everyday must improve.

The challenge is that most of us do not know WHO we are, and therefore do not know how to control our mental focus. In fact, most of us focus on what is not working and spent most of her energy focusing on what we DON'T want by asking questions like, "how come this always happens to me?" If you focus on that enough then that is what you will continue to experience. (Universal laws don't work unless you reprogram).

I am going to show you how to refocus your mental energy and reprogram your subconscious, so that you can ask better questions and therefore get a better result. Whatever you focus on, you manifest, which is why the Law of attraction won't work until you know what you want at the deepest level of your mind.

The key is to get you to live by those factors. Most people focus on the small stuff. I know you are to believe this, or you would not have picked up this book. Most people are so focused on what they have to DO. In other words, they focus on their to-do list, how to make a living instead of how to create their life. You could so easily get caught up in the day-to-day experiences that you tend to make a monument of the port in your mind, when actually in the long term these things that seem monumentally important now are actually quite trivial.

To create your masterpiece, you have to learn how to take care of the big things -- each color in your crayon box -- mentally, emotionally, physically, financially, and spiritually. Here are two things that usually lead to ultimate success -- either inspiration or desperation. Desperation can be a good thing because until you get really dissatisfied. You won't do anything to take your life to another level. Dissatisfaction is awesome! If you are completely satisfied, you will get comfortable. They may life begins to deteriorate.

My guess is that you invested in this book because on some level you are dissatisfied.

("If you make enough money, at least you can handle your problems in style" R)

(lots of money, beyond comfort zone)

"It's a funny thing, the more I practice the luckier I get" AP

Subconsciously, most of us have an idea of what we think we deserve. This is our comfort zone, which the subconscious mind determines when it sets our internal thermostat. Your subconscious mind has set your internal thermostat, and so when you begin to achieve, perhaps make a lot of money, you begin to sabotage your success in drop down to where you subconsciously think you deserve to be.

The past does not equal the future. Even if you are jaded and cynical, you've tried everything, this moment is a great new opportunity if you've tried other programs in the past that nothing has really changed your lifelong term. I believe that all it has done is it has prepared you for this program. And at some level if you did not believe that, then you would not be reading this right now.

Life Masterpiece is very different from other programs you may have tried. You will not find affirmations and visualizations and motivations in this book. What you will find is the answer to what is keeping you back, and how to reprogram your subconscious mind and how to use it to create

Your brain is the most powerful computer on the planet. When you learn to use it properly, you can create any result you want. And they can give you the answer to almost any problem you have. The problem is that this computer, we call our brain is not user-friendly, and does not come with an owner's manual. Life Masterpiece will show you how to operate your supercomputer with precision. Lasting change is not created in your life by learning more. Lasting change is created by using your own power to take action.

We're going to recondition the way your mind works by reprogram your subconscious. This will change the way you feel and the way you behave for the rest of your life. Just as there have been extraordinary technological, scientific and medical breakthroughs in the past two decades there has also been a breakthrough in the science of quantum physics. While we are not going to learn specifically about quantum physics in this book, we are going to take and use part of that technology. Because the latest cutting-edge tools for creating lasting change comes from breakthroughs in quantum physics that have to do with human technology and how to get new results in record time.

There are four steps to success:

1. Know what you want. It is important for you to know what you want, and for you to know how you want things to turn out. In other words, you must know your outcome before you begin. The first step is to decide what you want out of whatever situation you are currently in. The clearer you aren't what you want, the more you will empower your brain to give you the answers.

2. You must use it. In other words, you must get yourself to take action toward your outcome. This means that you must put energy in the right direction, even when you do not know exactly what to do. Many people do not know what to do first. I will teach you exactly what to do. Some people want to know what happens if they try, and it doesn't work. I can tell you right now, and you will learn why in this book, why nothing you try will ever work. So how do you take action? Decide to. It's not about what you can do. It's about what you will do.

3. Notice your results. It's not enough to take action. You must also pay attention to the results you are getting from your actions. Do your actions always work? No. Remember, success is just a series of failures, but failures with the purpose, failures directed at a specific result. You know what you want; you took action, now notice the result. (JS-obstacles and timing).

4. Be flexible and willing to change your approach. You must be willing to make changes and adjustments based on the results of your actions, because flexibility is the key to the system. In other words, if you notice that what you are doing is not working. And you're not getting closer to your goal or even getting further away, instead of feeling like a failure in giving up. Sometimes you simply need to change your approach.

There is a way to speed this up. Instead of just knowing what you want, taking random actions, I will show you a way to increase the pace and the certainty of your success.

("Knowledge is not power. Knowledge is potential power." R)

You may be thinking, "Jim, if this is a simple, how come everyone isn't doing it?" The answer is because the majority of people tend to get caught up in the day-to-day trivialities such as paying their bills. Now, paying your bills might seem monumentally important to you, but honestly, can you think of anyone who has ever reported that they were successful in life because they mastered the art of bill paying? I am not saying that you shouldn't pay your bills, what I'm saying is that you should know I yourself to get caught up in something trivial and make it something big, so that you can use it as an excuse for not doing the really important things in life. At the end of your life, no one is going to remember whether or not you paid all of your bills and what a wonderful job you did of it. In other words, people get caught up in making a living instead of creating a life. They come to the end of their life dissatisfied because they realize they only live 10% of it, not because they were not capable or intelligent, and not for a lack of knowledge, but simply because they never had a clear idea about what they wanted.

Some people think that what they really want is a program that deals with only one area of your life like that business program. If that is what you are thinking, let me tell you right now that Life Masterpiece is one of the most powerful business programs because it deals with the source of all your business -- YOU. When you are better will be a better speaker, salesperson negotiator. Your creativity will flow freely. Mobile to manage and influence people far more effectively than you can now. The first step to changing your career and your business is to change yourself.

***

www.lutesinternational.com

info@lutesinternational.com

https://www.facebook.com/jimlutes

https://mindmotionacademy.com

Anthony F. Navarro

Anthony Navarro is the creator of the Sabre Trading System, a method of locating opportunities in the financial markets for short-term income and long-term wealth. However, that wouldn't have been possible if Anthony had done what was "expected" of him instead of taking "the road less travelled."

As both trader and trainer, he teaches his proprietary methodology to his "Crew" at Sabre Trading Systems, which spans 30+ countries. His daily passion is to share his simple rules-based method in a visual, hands-on environment to achieve consistent, positive results by eliminating emotion-based trading and replacing bad habits with empowering beliefs.

Anthony is a featured author on the trader education website TradingView.com, has produced numerous educational videos and articles, and enjoys sharing his passion for trading on podcasts and associated media.

A dedicated advocate of self-improvement, Anthony has worked with the Tony Robbins Companies as a participant and coach at numerous international events. In addition, Anthony is active in Toastmasters International, serving various local and state leadership positions, and is passionate about helping people develop their leadership skills through public speaking and financial skills via trading.

When Anthony is not in front of a webcam, writing, or speaking, he enjoys watching movies in his home theater, zipping across the lake on his JetSki, cooking amazing meals on his kamado smoker, cycling, poker, and BeatSaber.

Because I Choose to

By Anthony F. Navarro

One of the most familiar lines in poetry belongs to Robert Frost's "The Road Not Taken:"

Two roads diverged in a wood, and I—

I took the one less traveled by,

And that has made all the difference.

I have encountered many such roads in life, and indeed, the direction I took **has** made all the difference. These roads share a similar quality: you can veer left and do what all your friends and family are doing, with the promise of a 'safe' and 'secure' life (whatever *that's* supposed to mean!), or veer right and do something bold. Something brave. Something you know people secretly **wish** they could do but are afraid to do. Sound familiar?

"It's too risky," they say. "You have no experience," they implore. And sometimes, underneath the veneer of compassionate concern, the little imp sneers, "Who do you think you are, you big dreamer? What? Do you think you're *better* than us? Know your place. Get back in formation!"

I hope that while I share some of my personal experiences of when and, more importantly, *how* I took the road less travelled, I might inspire you to "veer right" the next time life throws a forked road your way. Or better yet, don't wait for the road to appear; *build your own road!*

Most of us live a life of obscurity and safety which overrides our innate sense of adventure and purpose. "I was made for something *better* than this" is our heart's cry. So why do we follow the herd rather than blaze our own trail? Fear of failure? Fear of loss? Fear of success? (Crazy, right?) In times like these, your subconscious mind might be your worst enemy.

As a child, I dreamed of becoming an astronaut. I was a 'geek' long before the word was ever used to describe the modern technophile. Then life "went sideways" – my parents divorced, and my family fell apart. The college fund became the family legal fund. As is common in the life of a child of divorce, I had a **choice**: I could *succumb* to the hand I was dealt, or I could *succeed* in moving forward despite my circumstances. Consciously or subconsciously, at the time, I 'chose' to **not** let my family's fallout interfere with my childhood dream.

I **chose** to enroll in the aerospace program of our local college and **chose** to support myself financially with a "whatever it takes" attitude. As my studies began, the first space shuttle disaster occurred, which started the slow downward spiral of the aerospace industry. I said to myself, "Self, it sure would be nice if, after graduating college, I would actually have a *career* after investing all this time and money into my education!"

So while the aerospace industry was waning, the internet was becoming a thing. (Are you old enough to remember the days **before** the internet?) I was at another fork in the road. Again, I veered right. I changed my major to Computer Science. The internet was in its infancy, and green computer screens were all the rage! So instead of going to the moon as planned, I was exploring the 'strange new worlds' of digital technology right here on Earth.

Back then, universities were literal Petri dishes of innovation. (Today they're still Petri dishes but of a very different sort!) As part of my plan to support myself, I landed a job at the university, where I was exposed to amazing amounts of technology while gaining valuable project management experience. After three years, I had more hands-on experience as a 'network engineer' through my part-time job than most people twice my age with advanced degrees.

Another fork: an opportunity came my way to work in Manhattan as part of a three-person team tasked to overhaul a company's I.T. infrastructure. So, do I keep to the left and finish my education as all my friends, family, and guidance counselors told me to do, or do I 'veer right' and let 19-year-old me take advantage of this great opportunity? Of course, I veered right, against all the "sound advice" I received, and *"that has made all the difference."* That **one** decision allowed me to ride an incredible wave early in my career, and I seemed to "have it all" in terms of what one could want in my field.

And then I didn't.

After fifteen years under my belt, I didn't want to work for "a company" anymore. It was the age of striking it out on your own. And what happened? You guessed it: I came upon a fork in the road: I was laid off! So, do I veer left and get another "solid job" with a "solid company" (with 'solid' benefits?), or do I risk striking it out on my own once again?

You guessed correctly: I veered right.

I decided to start my business building websites. Had I ever built a commercial website? No. Had I ever had my own business with paying clients? No. Did I **choose** never to be forced to exchange time for money in a cubicle ever again? *Yes!*

Pink slip in hand, I went down the street to purchase a laptop, a printer, and blank business card stock. I was going to be a web designer. Learning how websites worked back when the technology was still in its infancy was like building a bridge while driving across it at 60 miles per hour! Yes, Google existed, but it wasn't anything like the helpful hive-mind we enjoy today.

Once I got my rhythm, I thrived on solving my customer's website needs while engaging my creativity – it hit all my hot buttons! I enjoyed my career as a web designer for about ten years, until it got to the point that I was spending more time fixing broken websites because of buggy software updates and hackers than I was building them. The joy, once again, was gone.

What to do next? Ideally, I wanted to earn my living from home, have a flexible schedule, not depend on customers, avoid hackers, say goodbye to commuting, and preferably not work in the computer field. I was tired of the never-ending cycle of installing, fixing, and upgrading things as I had for the last twenty years. I looked high and low for the next chapter in my professional life.

And, you guessed it… I veered to the right.

I **chose** to learn how to trade the financial markets. It again hit all my hot buttons. As word got around about my latest "career choice," I predictably had family and friends 'kindly suggest' that I consider a more 'traditional' career to pay my bills and support my family. This time, however, I also received outright ridicule, admonishment, and actual *hostility* regarding my decision! "So, I hear you're doing this trading thing." "Don't you know it's a rigged system?" "Trading is like gambling – the odds are against you!" "What, do you think you can beat the market or the 'Big Boys' on the inside?" "Do you really think that you, a 'computer guy' with no experience in the financial industry, can 'beat the market' when people who have been doing this for years and have fancy degrees can't even do it?" And most frustratingly: "Why take the risk?"

Why? Because I *choose* to.

It was **imperative** now that I pursued this path. Productivity guru Michael Hyatt said, "Anything worthwhile is opposed." So, I figured I had to be on the right track! If the universe was throwing this much flak at me to prevent me from doing it, it must be a test, a challenge to me, indicating that I *had* to do it.

As a hardcore movie fan(atic), I was reminded of a scene from *The Matrix Revolutions* when Agent Smith kept beating Neo down, but Neo refused to **stay** down. Finally, frustrated by Neo's unwillingness to "just be a good boy and die," Agent Smith, in exasperation, gave his "Why" monologue:

Agent Smith: "Why, Mr. Anderson? Why, why? Why do you do it? Why, why get up? Why keep fighting? You must know it by now. You can't win. It's pointless to keep fighting. Why, Mr. Anderson? Why? **Why** do you **persist**?"

Neo: "Because I **choose** to."

One of the most powerful things I have learned about motivation is that it sometimes presents itself **negatively**, as in, "I will achieve this goal so I will *never* have to work for someone else ever again."

My primary motivation to become a successful trader now also expressed itself in the negative: *"Prove Them Wrong."* I became **viscerally** determined to show my naysayers that, *yes*, I would succeed in becoming a trader. The first thing I did was print a poster that hung at eye level across my desk that read that very phrase: *"Prove Them Wrong."* And eventually, I did!

When the pandemic lockdowns spread across the globe, I realized I couldn't keep my knowledge to myself. I was now **compelled** to help others learn how to "put their money to work" because they weren't permitted to work, open their businesses, provide for their families, or in some cases, even leave the house to go shopping! In response I started an online academy where I enjoy the distinct privilege of teaching people how to trade the financial markets in a fun, interactive apprenticeship-style environment.

So, Dear Reader, we've now come to the place in the narrative where I'm supposed to share what I believe are the most effective ways that you too can **choose** to **do** what you want to do and **get** what you want to get out of life.

Step 1: Mirroring and Modeling

The achievement of success isn't 'rocket surgery.' It is simply, "Do what successful people do – get what successful people got." That's it! This can apply to anything from weight loss to relationship goals, to learning a skill (such as trading!).

For example, I stepped on the scale one morning and was shocked at the readout: I was a 268-pound hot mess! My heart cried, "How did I get this heavy?" Something clicked in me to finally **choose** to change. I dove onto the internet (which today is full of helpful information on virtually **any** topic) and searched for people who lost considerable amounts of weight safely, effectively, and realistically. I read their stories, came up with my own personal plan, "doing what they did, and getting what they got," losing 60 pounds of fat in six months – ten pounds per month – *like clockwork.*

Similarly, when I decided to become a trader, I sought the most successful people I could find who followed a systematic, rules-based trading plan that I could **emulate** and **replicate**. "Good artists copy and great artists steal," right? I sought out trader after trader creating step-by-step instructions on how to trade, and developed my system, which has, as Robert Frost would say, "made all the difference." I "did what my mentors did" and "got what my mentors got."

Here's your first assignment:

Ask yourself, "**Who** can I model, or what kind of person do I need to **seek out** and model that is **already** successful doing what I want to do? How can I learn their 'secret sauce' and make it my own, doing what they do so I can get what they've got?"

Step 2: Associate with those who have what you want.

It is said that a person is the average of the sum of the five people they are most closely associated with. In other words, "you are who you hang out with." So, if you are the most intelligent person in the room, you need to find another room! You need to associate with a group of people that will raise you up, not keep the status quo.

When I decided to lose weight, I chose to follow the "keto" system. So, naturally, I needed to find a community of fellow "Ketonians" to become associated with. I joined two keto Facebook communities, collected a handful of recipes, and created a routine to emulate and check in each day to encourage and be encouraged.

The same went for trading. I couldn't find a local group of traders, so I created my own on MeetUp.com which attracted over 100 members in very short order. We met every month to compare notes and share strategies. I absorbed as much as possible from those "smarter than me" and torture-tested every method I found. After some time, I discovered the person who would become my mentor. I joined his trading group and traded live with him three times per week. I learned his strategy, followed it to the letter, practiced thousands of trades, and made it my own. Like Neo taking the "red pill" in the Matrix, I eventually "saw what I needed to see," then I "did what I needed to do," and finally was "getting what I wanted to get."

Your second assignment:

What groups/individuals do I need to start associating with, and what groups/individuals might I need to step away from, if only for a season? There's nothing wrong with poker night, but if you're playing poker three nights per week (like I was!), how is that bringing you closer to your goal? (Unless your goal, of course, is to become a professional poker player.)

Step 3: Analyze, Execute, Evaluate – Then Rinse and Repeat.

Socrates is credited as saying, "The unexamined life is not worth living." You may be very busy working on your plan, but are you making actual **progress**? Here are three steps to make sure you are continually moving forward with your plan:

3.1. ANALYZE:

If your goal is to lose weight or be more fit, how do you know you are making progress? You must **track it**. How would you know that your trading system is working? You guessed it: you must **track it**.

For example, you can eat the healthiest foods but unwittingly be in caloric excess and not lose weight. If your goal, as mine was, was to lose 60 pounds in 6 months, we have to break it down: To lose

- 10 pounds of fat per month, you need to lose

- 2.5 pounds of fat per week, which contains

- 8,750 calories, which equals

- 1,250 calories per day.

3.2. EXECUTE:

The average daily caloric requirement is about 2,500 calories per day. Take away 1,250 calories and the daily caloric intake to achieve the goal is 1,250 calories, or 416 calories per meal if you eat three meals daily. To **execute** this, you could, for example, portion your food in advance in 400-calorie portioned containers to "grab and go" throughout the week.

3.3. EVALUATE:

What if I wanted to splurge while out at dinner with friends? I could enjoy a more extensive meal of 800 or 1200 calories, skip one of the smaller meals, and make it an intermittent fasting day. I would continue to tweak as needed. Did I cheat? What could I do to prevent that from happening again? ...and so on. To paraphrase Socrates, "The diet not analyzed is not worth following."

3.4. RINSE AND REPEAT:

Continual refinement, or what Tony Robbins calls CANI *(Constant and Never-Ending Improvement)*, is the system's key. With each Evaluation phase, make any necessary changes and repeat your plan.

Your third assignment:

Find or create a **system** that will get you to your goal. Develop a **measurable** plan that you can evaluate weekly, if not daily. Then put measures in place where you can stick to your plan.

Step 4: Focus Like a Laser

A five-watt light bulb doesn't do much. You could use one for a night light so you don't stub your toe in the middle of the night. Take those five watts, however, and put them into a *laser*, and you can cut through steel! It's the **same** amount of light. It's simply a matter of **focus**. The phrase "Jack of all trades and the master of none" reflects this truth: You can do ten things poorly, three things adequately, or one thing at an *impressive* level of excellence.

I tell all the members of my trading group: If you backtest 100 trades per day to learn our system, you will get to a level of competence much faster than someone who trains "when they have the time." Whatever your goal, you will never 'find the time'… you must *make* the time. Ask yourself, "Do you want to be a **laser** or a light bulb?"

Your fourth assignment:

What can you identify that takes time in your life that you can temporarily or permanently eliminate so you may **focus** your efforts on your goal like a **laser**?

For example, your weekly bowling group may get a permanent ban on your time, but participation in a civic or professional organization like Toastmasters can perhaps be sidelined for three to six months while you focus on achieving your goal. Set a target date or sequence of milestones to create a sense of urgency!

Step 5: Pass On What You Have Learned

One of the best ways to learn is to **teach**. I have a friend who also wanted to trade. While developing my system, I mentored him regularly. It not only helped my friend but made my system more effective through continual improvements. As I mentioned earlier, I later created *Sabre Trading Systems* to teach others my methodology, which has blessed people in over 30 countries. Thanks to teaching, my simple trend-based system can now locate opportunities in all types of trading environments. I would *never* have been able to do this without teaching what I know to others.

Your final assignment:

While pursuing your goal, figure out how you could positively impact others by sharing your passion, system, or story. Dream big, be bold, and don't be afraid to "veer right" **today**.

Where will the path on your right take you?

What step will you take towards your dream today *…because you choose to?*

***

To Contact Anthony:

Website: http://SabreTradingSystems.com

Website: http://AnthonyNavarro.com

eMail: anthony.navarro@icloud.com / anthony@sabretradingsystems.com

Phone: 704-777-9585

FaceBook: https://www.facebook.com/AnthonyFNavarro

Twitter: https://twitter.com/AnthonyFNavarro

LinkedIn: https://www.linkedin.com/in/ocaptain/

Misty Blakesley

Misty Blakesley is trained Healer and meta cognitive expert who teaches the importance of integrating your spiritual practice and personal magic into the real world so that you can restore your birthright to love, abundance, prosperity, and wealth. By combining her spiritual gifts with science, Misty helps her clients achieve lasting results

In addition to being a published author and public speaker, Misty founded Lemonade with Love where she offers group and one-on-one life coaching.

Misty lives with her husband, Bill, their son, Liam, and two fur babies, Ty and Stella, in her dream home complete with outdoor oasis in Cumming, GA. Her hobbies include spending time in nature and tending her gardens. She also loves to entertain family and friends with delicious food, amazing drinks, and intriguing conversation. And best of all, Misty loves making memories with her family.

My Journey to Becoming

by Misty Blakesley

My face is soaked with tears. It's cold outside but I am sweating. I am stuck in this car, riding four and half hours to North Carolina to see my sister, nieces, and mom. Three hours in and I have been sobbing the entire time. I mean ugly crying, the kind of crying where your entire body is shaking, your nose is running, and your face is contorted. I have another hour and half left to my trip and there is no end in sight to these tears. My heart is broken, it is shattered, and I don't know how to fix it.

It's been three months. Three months since my world was turned upside down. This isn't like me. I always "fix" things. I fix my things, and come to think of it, I fix everyone else's things too. I am a "pick yourself up, fix your makeup, and power through" kind of girl. Why is it so hard this time? Why are my methods not working?

You see, three months ago, I lost the promise of my little girl, my Sara Jane. With devastating news, my pregnancy ended at sixteen weeks and my husband, and I lost our little girl and the promise of what we believed that meant for us. Pink bows and ballet. Lots of frilly clothes and a Daddy's girl. We were both grieving for what we had lost and the way we had lost it.

I allow myself a couple of weeks to process and accept what has happened and then it is back to work. I hide my pain. I don't want anyone to know how bad it still hurts. I will dry my eyes and pull it together, so my family won't see. So that no one sees, not even my husband.

The trip home from North Carolina was just the same, four-and-a-half hours of intense emotion and heart wrenching, soul crushing sobs. It was during that drive, however, that my life would change forever. It was in those moments that I realized that I needed help, that I was not going to find my way through this alone. It was in this moment and from this situation, that I would start my journey to a type of healing and a level of healing I never knew was possible. It would be the start of something amazing, even though there was no way I could see it in those moments.

Once I had complete awareness that I wasn't going to make it through this trauma without help, I set the intention that I would do just that. I had no idea who or where. What I did know, is that I wasn't interested in clinical therapy. I had been down that path earlier in my life, and it left me more confused and frustrated than when I started. And, more importantly, I knew what I did want, soul level, life-changing healing.

The most wonderful thing about the universe is that when you set an intention with as much emotion and conviction as I had that day, it has no choice but to answer. All that is required of us is to keep an open mind and receive inspired action.

In this process, I have learned acquiring knowledge of energy and spiritual healing isn't just for healers or those wanting to become healers. This work is for everyone! This knowledge will send you down a path to creating the life you always desired. I use all of my knowledge to create tangible and physical success in my personal and professional life.

For me and my work, it is important that others recognize that spiritual knowledge isn't separate from worldly knowledge. And spiritual work isn't separate from worldly work. The key is integrating the spiritual into the physical, manifesting real and tangible results like meaningful relationships, children, your dream house, a fulfilling career or calling, immense amounts of money in your bank account, and more!

If you are brand new to this journey, or have been on this road for some time, there are three profound lessons that I wish to share:

First, this journey is yours alone.

Second, setting strong boundaries is critical for your healing and growth.

Third, money work is never about the money.

When I first discovered all that is energy healing, I was blown away. And, like most people, when we stumble upon profound, life-changing knowledge, we want to share it with everyone we love and care about. We begin telling our partners, spouses, siblings, and closest friends. And as we experience life change after life change, tangible result after result, our desire to bring those closest to us along increases exponentially.

For me, the person I most desired to bring along was my husband. I thought, "If I can create these kinds of results by myself, imagine what we could achieve if we did this together!" I know many of you are like, "YES! That is my thought exactly." And like many of you, I tried and tried to "encourage" him to join in. To say he was not interested in the least is an understatement. My ongoing effort led to a lot of frustration and tension for me and the person I love the most. I am grateful that he has what seems to be never-ending patience for me. In this experience, my husband was the teacher. He taught me that it is possible to share an incredible bond, love, and life, while experiencing very separate journeys. He has always given me space to explore every aspect of myself, all the while showing me and my experiences, the highest level of support and respect. And, I found that when I provided him that same space, support, and respect, my room to explore grew, as did his.

The lesson here: **this journey is your own.** You cannot bring anyone with you. And the harder your try, the slower your progress becomes. This particular journey doesn't work this way. It's not like sharing a dream vacation or enjoying a five-star meal. And for this, I am most grateful, as this is the most personal journey you will ever take, diving into your closest held secrets, your deepest (and sometimes insidious) guilt and shame, and all those beliefs that hold you hostage.

What I now realize is that we all manifest wonderful and amazing experiences and material possessions in the most unique and personal way. My husband is a master manifester. He may not call it that. But he does create the life he wants, in the way that feels most natural to him.

When we allow everyone in our lives to grow, expand, love, and experience in their own time and in their own way, we begin to experience a beautiful unity, peace, and calm within. I encourage you to follow your inspiration when it comes to how and with whom you share your journey. You may choose to share information or keep it sacred. And do all of this knowing that the universe is always supporting you and your loved ones. The universe has a way of delivering all you desire without the direct participation of your loved ones. The universe continues to deliver to me over and over without requiring joint participation from my loved ones, even my husband.

Once I understood that this was my journey alone, I begin to understand that I am like a turtle, making my way to the vast sea where anything is possible, and where I can be, do, and have anything. And the quickest way to do that was to unload all those I had tried to carry on my back and take with me, to allow them to find their own way to the sea, knowing that we would all end up there eventually.

This is where things get interesting. You see, many knew me as the turtle. For thirty-five-plus years, they knew me this way. I played a role in their lives, a role they had come to depend on and that I had become quite comfortable with (although, not happy about). For some, I was a mediator. Some, a door mat. Others, a pushover. Don't misunderstand, not everyone in my life treated me in one of these ways. And I have my husband and a couple of very close friends that have always loved me in a very healthy way and have watched me morph into a very independent, boundary-rich, individual. It has been a very rewarding journey for me, and I enjoy the validation they provide when they express the ways they have seen me change, expand, and grow.

Setting boundaries in places where none have existed can be hard and trying. That being said, it is critical. And it is really important that you understand, boundaries are all about YOU, not others. This has been a decade long journey for me. And the toughest place to build boundaries for me was within my family.

I grew up with two sisters and both my parents until age thirteen, when my father passed away from cancer. We all played a role in this family unit, and these roles morphed and then amplified after the loss of my father. And these roles served us in some way at the time. That is the conundrum: since they served us then, most of us tend to take these familial roles with us into adulthood, where they very rarely continue to serve us. It is why so many of us dread holidays and other events that bring us all back together again, under one roof. For me, I continued to serve as the compliant mediator within my family. I was the one that placated everyone to keep peace. I was known as the peace maker. That role in and of itself isn't bad, until you compromise all of your personal desire for the "good of the group," to the point where you are no longer happy or enjoying yourself.

As I began to become the strong, independent, successful women I knew I could be, I began to implement boundaries. Doing this requires all those in my life to observe and respect the woman that I am now and that I continue to become. It requires those that have known me since birth to see me with a new lens. That is as much a journey for them as it has been for me. What I have learned is how to hold space full of love for those people, as they adjust to my new expectations for how I am to be treated and supported. For anyone experiencing this now or, maybe realizing this is a must next step, please remember to have grace for yourself and your loved ones. This journey tends to be a transition that happens over time, one boundary at a time. You will get there and so will your loved ones. The space between can be filled with times of non-communication, can feel like a hiatus, or simply feel a bit distant. Just know that the boundaries you set are absolutely worth it. You are worth it. And remember, the universe is always here to support us on our journey to self-love, enlightenment, and expansion. Especially when we do so from a place of absolute love.

The last message I wish to impart is about money. Why money? Because, in this humanly experience, on this planet, money is the energetically neutral (paper and naturally occurring metals) used to provide material goods (home, food, heat, electricity) and, most of all, FREEDOM. Another reason I believe this message is important is because it's the reason I hear most often for not investing in personal healing. When I started this journey, I wanted healing and a baby. And I got both, fast. And once I had him, I started to see the other areas in my life where I wanted more. More time, more money, more freedom. I wanted to be the best wife and mother I could be without sacrificing a career that also brought me fulfillment and joy. Having it all with complete balance seemed elusive at first. And, like my previous experience, once I begin to focus my awareness and healing around this desire, the universe delivered. In spades!

If you take nothing else away from the words I share with you in this text, please remember this, **your money story has nothing to do with money itself.** Let me say that again, YOUR MONEY STORY HAS NOTHING TO DO WITH MONEY ITSELF. Whether you are elbow deep in lack or standing on a wave of wealth you wish to take higher, your current money story is completely tied to your current belief system. And it's not just tied to your belief system about money, it is tied to your belief system about YOU. To make this even clearer, most of us start our healing journey, dropping a belief system that isn't even our own, but the system that was handed down to us by our parents, family, and church. And that belief system has been passed down from generation to generation. Most of us are holding onto belief systems that no longer serve us, simply because of the strength and depth of our commitment to the known and the paralyzing fear of the unknown. It's our fear of what might happen if we let go of all we know for the opportunity to explore many things we do not. Your fear is trying to protect you from getting hurt, but in reality, it is holding you hostage to the very things you are trying to escape.

My profound and confident belief in this truth is based on my own personal experiences. Letting go of the known to pursue the unknown is scary! And it is worth it! I encourage you to show yourself grace. And to do so, while you take a leap of faith, and jump into a journey that will forever change you and your reality for the better.

There were many times I invested in healing and coaching for myself, not knowing how all the money would come together. I have made that investment through credit cards and payment plans. Why did I invest? Because I craved the life of abundance. Deep down, I knew life didn't have to be hard. I could see it in examples all around me. I knew many that made six figure incomes working less than thirty-two hours a week. And I knew if they could achieve that, then so could I. I just didn't know how. So, I hired a teacher, a life coach, and a spiritual mentor. Almost a decade later, after experiencing exponential growth that led to expanding my money multiple times, I still invest in this. Why? Because denial is strong. If we are the only thing standing between the life we have now and the life we truly desire, then there are some hard truths hiding inside. It is impossible to see our blind spots without help. It is why vehicles have invested in adding technology to change that. And why is it so important to have someone or something that can see our blind spots? Because it can CHANGE and even SAVE our lives.

So, this memoir is dedicated to my Sara Jane. Thank you for setting me on a journey only sixteen weeks (of pregnancy) with you could have started. Thank you for blessing my life in ways I never knew would be possible even though you are on the other side. Thank you, my sweet baby girl, for all you inspire in me. And thank you for sending me Liam, the rainbow baby you knew my heart needed.

I no longer believe in coincidence. I believe all things are orchestrated based on our desires. And if you desire a new, abundant life, filled with all good things, then I believe that is why you are reading my words. If my journey is inspiring you, then take your inspired action, NOW! Don't wait, the life you crave is right in front of you. Invite a teacher into your life that can show you how to step into your love, abundance, prosperity, health, and wealth!

About the author:

Misty Blakesley is trained Healer and meta cognitive expert who teaches the importance of integrating your spiritual practice and personal magic into the real world so that you can restore your birthright to love, abundance, prosperity, and wealth. By combining her spiritual gifts with science, Misty helps her clients achieve lasting results

In addition to being a published author and public speaker, Misty founded Lemonade with Love where she offers group and one-on-one life coaching.

Misty lives with her husband, Bill, their son, Liam, and two fur babies, Ty and Stella, in her dream home complete with outdoor oasis in Cumming, GA. Her hobbies include spending time in nature and tending her gardens. She also loves to entertain family and friends with delicious food, amazing drinks, and intriguing conversation. And best of all, Misty loves making memories with her family.

***

To contact Misty:

Website: https://www.lemonadewithlove.com/

LinkedIn: https://www.linkedin.com/in/mistyblakesley/

Email: misty@lemonadewithlove.com

Nicole Ortiz

Nicole currently resides and practices in northern New Mexico, nestled among the Sangre de Cristo Mountains, a land possessing a rich heritage and history of healing. After serving in the United States Air Force Nicole embarked on a passion journey focused on growth and self-discovery. Along the way, she earned a Master's degree in Counseling from Southwestern College, in Santa Fe and opened The Santa Fe Institute of Holistic Coaching.

Nicole's clinical and research interests include interpersonal communication, trauma, and authenticity. She is actively sought out as a seminar leader, trainer and advisor. In addition to creating the FLY-HOME system, a coaching system designed to facilitate self-discovery while honoring authenticity, Nicole served as the Director of Clinical Services for one of the most renowned residential trauma programs in the United States.

Each day Nicole strives to lead a life rooted in love, respect, and self-acceptance. As her favorite poet, Walt Whitman once said, "Happiness, not in another place but this place… not for another hour, but this hour." Owning our happiness, staying present, and fostering growth are some of Nicole's core beliefs. She also believes you can have ownership over your unique experience; begin thriving in growth and cultivate happiness.

Love is a Funny Thing

By Nicole Ortiz

Love is a funny thing. What love means to one person can vary greatly from another. I would describe love very differently now than I would have 25 years ago. Having love for oneself can dramatically shift how we see ourselves and especially affect how we treat ourselves. I find this concept incredibly important to examine, because without love and respect for yourself how can you live a fulfilled, contented life? How can you do what best serves you and brings you joy? If you lack a true understanding of the definition of "self-love", how can you move past your flaws and allow yourself grace in your humanness?

Several years ago, I began working with clients as a therapist and life-coach. One of the first questions I ask clients is "Who are you?" and "How do you describe yourself?" In almost every instance client's either cannot answer the question, the resounding, "I don't know!" or they begin by describing themselves negatively, really focusing on what they are *not*. I made it my mission to understand the correlation between love and respect.

Almost all relationship issues, especially the internal relationship with the self, boils down to lack of respect profoundly shapes the way we love. Do you love yourself? Do you have the kind of respect you need to make loving decisions that will allow for the healthiest path for your life? The opposite of love is apathy. When we are not sitting in a loving internal space, we cannot envision life as an existence of bountiful peace and happiness. If we do not feel love we often feel that opposite mindset of indifference or not caring about our wellbeing.

I was recently listening to Tony Robbins speak about reaching your unlimited power. Tony used the metaphor of walking on hot coals to describe overcoming our most difficult obstacles; tapping into the unlimited potential we all possess. As a trauma specialist, someone who has worked deeply with people struggling with trauma and addiction, I believe you have already walked through fire. You may have overcome huge life moments to be where you are today, right now! You may not recognize what you have been through as "trauma" because you may not have had the therapeutic language to attach to it; but many experiences are traumatic, nonetheless. You are walking through hot coals in your mind. You are walking through the embers of life's challenges. Making it to the other side of that hot flaming pit of coals takes a certain level of strength and truth. The wisdom that life brings us when difficult circumstances drag us down to the ground. Bent so far that we are almost flat, lying face down in our circumstances.

You see none of this could be handled without some level of love and perseverance. We inherently possess internal motivators, or resilience, that keeps us together and moving forward. Respect for our strength in journey can be enough in our worst times to propel us forward, even if just an inch. An inch is progress. What motivates and propels you? I have a strong faith and belief in God. Faith that keeps me on track. Being a child of God allows me the space to embrace the difficulties and love the flawed aspects of self, that prior, brought me shame and self-loathing. I can now appreciate the gifts that have been afforded to me and walk-through darkness by keeping an eye on the light. I respect my journey and that creates space to love.

If you become really internally quiet can you begin to hear what you tell yourself? Are you having loving conversations with self? Or are you stuck in negative self-talk that is dragging you down? Is a lack of respect affecting how you love yourself? Or if we flip the perspective; Is a lack of love making it impossible to have any respect for yourself? Maybe love is not possible to reach at this point, maybe you can't even look at yourself in the mirror! So how do you begin? What will be the catalyst for change? Honestly you began reading this book; that is evidence of desire for change. Take small moments to appreciate what you can do right now. Your capacity to take on more will grow with your success.

I truly believe that you should celebrate even the smallest of successes. Any moment, no matter how small, should be acknowledged. This acknowledgement is a signal to the nervous system that you are experiencing something different, something positive, and you want to concretize this change. You will begin to solidify your new positive response by attaching a positive, loving feeling. Say it out loud, name it, write it down. Our minds are like computer programs, and we want to rewrite the software that goes offline whenever we experience a moment and do not react in a way that positively serves us. You want to equate love and respect. You must teach yourself that you are now serving your highest good. That means you love yourself, when you love yourself, you will respect yourself. When you respect yourself, you will make healthier choices.

Begin to narrow your focus. By doing this it allows you the clarity to see the path ahead that you are meant to be on, at this moment. Allow space for the path to shift. By staying flexible and traveling in fluidity you will not feel the pain of rigidity. Rigidity does not allow you change course, making mistakes feel like failures. You are a human, you will make human decisions, that is ok! It is all growth.

Adopt a narrower vision. A single focused vision helps you identify the one thing that draws all your attention, while simultaneously giving space to be in the experience. Now you may be thinking what's wrong with thinking broadly. A broad vision makes room for all my needs. However, when you self-examine with too broad a vision, you could become overwhelmed and that leads to focusing on the negatives. If you draw your focus in, narrowly, you can take your challenges on in a way that allows for completion, eliminates procrastination, and feels manageable.

We live in a multitask, microwave society – do more and do it faster! Operating like this is not only unsustainable, but it is unkind, and unloving. The internal message we send self is, "I don't respect your time and ability, so I don't love what you do!" So then how can you show yourself kindness and respect amidst the pressures to perform? Start by having respect for your experience. Show yourself love in the form of understanding your needs and hold boundaries.

Boundary setting is a simple, yet powerful way to show yourself, and others, that you have a deep respect for your experience. Create a vision of the life you wish to experience, then set boundaries to meet this expectation. This vision is the mental place where you take your normally chaotic thought processes and shift these thoughts to reflect internal peace. When you stop thinking about everything at once, no longer splitting your attention 20 different ways, you can then be more productive. You can shift your self-respect to show how much you love yourself. You are telling yourself that your time is a priority, and your thoughts are loving.

This begins the process of letting go of the negative defeating language. The thoughts that do not belong to you! The negativity that was dumped on you by a third-grade bully, an unkind angry parent, an ex-lover who was only interested in getting a reaction out of you in a heated moment. The good news is – those thoughts are not yours! Give them back! Get rid of the voice whispering in your ear that you are not good enough, flawed, broken, insert negative yuck here_____. Drop what is not yours and stop getting mentally hijacked by unwanted emotions. Who's driving your emotional bus? Are you stuffed in the trunk of your rapidly moving, emotional vehicle wishing you could contain all the nonsense that spills out when you don't believe you deserve good things? When you feel angry and hurt, unheard and unseen? You are allowing this lack of respect to form the way you love. This self-examination is not meant to feel blaming. It is the reality of surviving trauma, and self-love can help ease the suffering.

The good news is if it isn't yours or your voice then you no longer have to believe the lies that are limiting you. You have the power to love yourself enough to take back your experience. Put down that heavy, burdensome load and walk your path lighter in truth. When the negative limiting beliefs arise tell them, "Stop!", "No.", "Lies!", whatever phrase feels true to you. Make this the mantra that stops the disrespectful, unloving thoughts in their tracks, and when you get a good feel for the power of this small but weighty statement you can apply it to any and all ruminations that keep you stuck in a headspace of negativity.

Try to speak to yourself as you would to a small child you love, or an elder you have great respect for. Would you use that angry tone or hateful speech with them? Of course not! So why then do you speak to yourself harshly? It is easy to be unkind and unloving with ourselves, but let's remember all you have already endured and respect yourself for it. Have compassion for your internal wounds. Remember any negative experiences are a pit of scorching coals. Walk on those coals and own your experience. Self-love = self-respect and self-respect allows for an authentic, loving experience.

I have not always been peaceful, content, or even felt healthy at times. I grew up in a home that did not value children. A space of profound difficulty however gave birth to a thirst for knowledge and understanding of experience. This built resilience and made me a compassionate, empathetic student of the human condition… I love learning about people and fostering conversations of growth and healing. Working with patients has brought me a lot of stories that have intermingled with my own. It is important not to become stuck in the spiderweb.

When self-examining on a deep level it sometimes gets much harder before it becomes clear. Learning how to move through your darkness and difficulties can seem like pulling that one golden thread while attempting to untangle the entire web. You can't help but become painfully aware of the interweaving of the paths of others with your own. It is my belief that our early childhood experiences form the ways our nervous systems deal and cope with the world; the way you see your limitations and witness your growth is born in this place.

Potential is formed in those moments when your caregivers were unable to meet your needs. Whether intentionally or not, you learned to adapt to the situation. The less you are provided the more you must fill in the gaps. Your system had experiences, and those experiences taught you how to respond. You then formed an opinion of self-based upon the reaction of others. That is important because it set the tone for the quality of the relationship you were forming.

The way you coped was based upon the reaction you wanted to invoke. The reaction is largely controlled by the response and depends on understanding your role in the system. Understanding who you are and what you want to achieve is a huge piece of the equation. Of course, as small children, it is trial by fire. You can only be as healthy as the system itself. But as an adult you can take that hardwiring, claim the pieces that still serve you and reclaim the parts of self you do not love and respect. It becomes easy when you can answer one simple question… What do you want?

I work with so many clients who absolutely cannot answer that question. They have no idea what they want! So then, if you don't know what you want, how can you understand what you need? Are your needs the same as your wants? Do you end up with more questions than answers? If you don't know what makes you happy, how do you know how to get there? If you don't know the destination, how can you follow the map? The answer is incredibly simple… Happiness is a feeling state and feeling states are within making contentment internal; it cannot be achieved externally. Nothing you buy, no relationship you build, substance you use, or place you go can produce this result. You must stop and reflect; how can you measure contentment? When you truly love and accept that authentic version of self will it be enough?

The good news is only you can tell when you have reached your goals and objectives. Which means you do not have to worry about judgement. This is a personal journey. Life is a personal journey. When you stop putting your definitions of love and respect in the hands and hearts of others you take back the ownership of the authentic experience. Authenticity is powerful because it is expressed only by the author of the experience. You are the narrator of your story. You may choose to travel alongside other characters, but you are the protagonist!

When you are able to take inventory of the journey and feel good about the choices and outcomes you will feel content. Dare I say even happy? Yes! You will feel what you see others experiencing; that state of being that always seemed just out of reach. When you practice meeting your needs, out of respect for your own experience in the world, you can't help but feel loved. You will learn to rewire the love-centers of your mind and turn the negative speech to words of respect. Self-worth grows in this space, you will no longer grapple with the question, "Do I deserve love?". We all deserve love, especially from ourselves. When you walk in the energy of love and respect you teach others how to love you. You give off a vibe of positivity and that is hard to deny. Have you ever met someone that you just wanted to know? What was it about them that drew you in? That is the undefinable positivity gene; not provided by your parents DNA but grown in your consciousness and manifested by ownership of your unique experience.

The last point I wish to touch upon is the power of true acceptance. By sitting in complete acceptance of your past you will destroy any fear or anxiety. What I mean is, if you spend your precious minutes worrying about "mistakes" or "bad decisions" there can be no growth. You cannot stay stuck in the past while moving forward into the future, the two cannot exist together. You must make peace with what has propelled you to get to this crucial point and give grace and forgiveness for being human. You are in constant flux. That is exciting! Become excited at each new opportunity to fine tune your skills. All lessons are just that, meant to teach what to do or *not* do moving forward. By staying stuck in the mud of unforgiving and lack of acceptance you do not respect the truth in your experience. You do not love yourself as you are.

The difficult moments and "bad" choices are the battle scars that built your capacity to understand what not to do next time! Acceptance is a beautiful showing of love and respect. That ever-growing self will foster faster development. It is sitting in shame that depletes our confidence and beats us out of developing to our fullest version of self. Think back to your childhood, did you respond and grow faster with praise or criticism? Were you positively driven by coaches that rode you hard? Or by teachers that encouraged you in adversity? You are your own teacher; you can find the answers! Together we can keep searching for the best questions to suit your growth and needs.

With the knowledge of what respect, love, acceptance, success, wants, and needs mean to you, you will be armed with the tools you need to take on not only your past experiences; but to gain the advantage over your present and future. Spend some time thinking and/or journaling about the following questions:

1. Who am I?
2. What do I need to feel content, happy, safe, and whole?
3. What does authenticity mean to me and how do I know when I am being my true self?
4. What do I want to leave behind, so others know I have been here?
5. Do I love myself? Why or why not….
6. How can I show myself love?
7. Do I accept myself? Why or why not?
8. How can I grow my acceptance?
9. Do I respect myself? Why or why not?
10. How can I show myself respect?
11. What are my values?
12. Is it important to live in my value system?
13. Do I need to examine my boundaries with others?
14. Do I need to examine my boundaries with myself?
15. How can I grow and foster my inner peace?

Self-respect is the internal scaffolding you need to stay erect when you feel like caving in, and self-love is the armor that protects your heart and soul from penetrating arrows of hurt during the toughest battles. You can travel the roughest roads when fueled by love and respect. You have been through hardships, but you have gained wisdom. Keep trusting in your internal knowledge of self and know your merit. Love is a funny thing, it means many things to many people, you only need to define it to yourself. Search for love from within and keep traveling. Self-respect comes with time, allow yourself to heal and grow, give space for grace, and enjoy the heat of the coals that are fueling the beauty of all journeys.

To contact Nicole:

www.iamnico-o.com

email: iamnicoo@outlook.com

Instagram: thenico.o

Twitter: @iamnico_o

Craig Wayne Boyd

Rooted in the southern tradition of country music and topped with a rebellious flair, Craig is an extreme talent who excelled at singing and playing the guitar at age of four. He received long-due critical and mainstream recognition as the Season 7 winner of The Voice. Taking the title as a member of Team Blake (Shelton), Craig dazzled the audience with the premiere performance of "My Baby's Got A Smile on Her Face," which debuted #1 on the Hot Country Songs chart, becoming the second song (following Garth Brooks' "More Than A Memory") to ever do so.

Growing up in the Dallas, Texas suburb of Mesquite, Craig's childhood was highly influenced by gospel and country music and he later became the choir director at his hometown church. After a trip to Nashville, life-changing events came his way. Craig signed a publishing deal with EMI and after several years of prolific songwriting, he began touring heavily, logging more than 1,000 shows in four years, and opening for acts like Jamey Johnson, Randy Houser and Brantley Gilbert. In 2015, Craig opened up for Rascal Flatts during their *Vegas Riot!* nine-show residency at the Hard Rock Casino in Las Vegas before continuing on his headlining *West Bound and Down Tour*.

I'm Still Here

By Craig Wayne Boyd

"Life is made up of all these tidbits. What you do with them, and how you use them, is what dictates the rest of your life, so concentrate on the small things" ~ Bob Spear

A wise man named Bob Spear once told me, ***"Life is made up of all these tidbits; what you do with them and how you use them, is what dictates the rest of your life, so concentrate on the small thing"***. For me, those tidbits always had something to do with music. It's always been a part of me. I grew up surrounded by music... whether I was singing in my church choir, school plays, listening to music or completely devoting myself to learning the instruments I picked up at garage sales. I knew music was in my future because I couldn't get enough of it. Which musical path to take was something I struggled with early in my life. As the son of a honky-tonk player and a mother who raised me to sing gospel. I was constantly conflicted until the pastor of my church, explained to me that you can't always preach to the choir and to go where I was led.

I wasn't sure what all of that meant until I was 23. My father and I travelled to Nashville where I was fortunate enough to meet a very prominent person in the music publishing scene and play a few songs for him that I'd written in Dallas. He told me I was on the right track but that I had to be present to win and then he asked if I was willing to move to Music City and start a new journey. I never thought twice about it. I said *"Yes"* surprising myself with no hesitation. On the way home I looked up and said, *"God, is this what I'm really supposed to do?"*

> *We can sometimes question ourselves out of our dreams, not realizing it. After all, I'd just built a new house, I was married & I had a stable six figure job... was I going to do this and did it even make sense? The answer came to me like a 2x4 across the forehead when I pulled up to my house and found a note from my then wife. She had left me along with specific instructions not to try to find her.*

Shortly thereafter I became extremely depressed. I lost my sales job and one rainy night in Texas, I rolled and totaled my truck. Being told I was lucky to be alive, I wasn't feeling very *lucky* but I knew that God had given me my answer. Six months later, I was on my way to Nashville with everything I could pack in the back of an old farm truck my father had loaned me.

After moving to Nashville, it seemed as if I was on my way to fulfilling my dream. I was writing with some great songwriters, performing in writers' rounds, and formed the trio, Southland, with musicians Cole Lee and Levi Sims. A year later I landed a publishing deal with EMI, one of the most renowned publishing companies in the world. For 3 years, life was good. The trio was getting positive attention, we had labels interested in us, and we were playing packed venues. You know if there's one thing the music industry will teach you, over and over again... don't hold your breath. Before I knew it, my trio had broken up, I had lost my publishing deal, and close friend and former band mate, Levi, had passed away from cystic fibrosis. I was back to square one, grieving the loss of my friend, and trying to figure out how to pick up the pieces. Bob's words would swim through my head, "tidbits, and what you do with them, concentrate on the small things". I hung on to these words.

After much contemplation I decided to pursue a solo career. I took the heartache of the last few years into the studio and recorded an album to reflect the highs and lows of my life. I found new band members and hit the road... playing gigs from Minot, North Dakota to Key West, Florida and everywhere in between. I was introduced to a new independent label in Nashville and we recorded another album to reflect the *determination* that I had to finish what I started. The single from that album was a direct reflection of my journey so far; aptly titled, **"I Ain't No Quitter"**. We even made a video and submitted the single to radio where it began climbing the charts. Finally, I was back! The single reached the top 30's on the Music Row Charts, defying the precedent at the time that if you weren't on a major label, it was nearly impossible to get a song played. I was determined to break the Nashville mold and be an independent artist with a hit single. I'd been playing nearly 250 dates a year, including a radio tour where I visited every radio station that would have me.

And don't hold your breath again! When I returned from one of my radio tours, I saw movers pulling furniture out of my independent label's office. My immediate thought was, "Awesome! We're getting new furniture", but the reality was that the company had lost its funding. Even with my single still moving up the charts, I was headed back to square one once again.

> *No label, no money to pay band members, no gigs and back to the drawing board. It was 2012, strike three.*

I'm not sure if it was my "stupidity" or "stick-to-itiveness" that kept me going, but I know most sane people would have packed it in and given up. By now, I was a new father to my first child, a son Jaxon, who had become a new inspiration in my life. It wasn't just about me anymore and I had the pressing responsibility to be successful and do what I knew to do to support him. My current single, *"I Ain't No Quitter"*, was supposed to define me and yet there I was, standing at a crossroads, trying to decide if I had the strength to move forward. The answer was yes, because ***I was not a quitter and I would find a way figure it out***. I started over again and for 2 years I played as many gigs that I could on the road, supplementing income wherever I could to support my son. I picked up jobs working construction while also writing and performing as often as possible. I will never forget this one day in particular, I was working on a job site when a Nashville label executive came into the house we were building and recognized me. He looked at me and asked, "Aren't you Craig Wayne Boyd, what are you doing here?" I told him I had a son to support now and needed to pick up some extra work. I've never been ashamed of who I am, and don't get me wrong, hard work has never beneath me, but in this moment I truly felt defeated. This isn't where I wanted to be, it was where I had to be.

> *I began questioning God's plan for me... was music really the route I was intended to pursue? Had I already used up all of my chances or was there another lesson, another road I had travel to find my way?*

My landlord had just given me 30 days to move out and it seemed like I was being pushed in another direction. Nearly homeless and out on the road, I'd just had a heart to heart with my drummer about quitting music and concentrating on another career. I didn't want to give it up, but I needed something stable so I could confidently support my son. With quitting on my mind, I opened up my computer, only to find an email from a producer of the NBC TV show The Voice, asking if I would be interested in auditioning for season 7 of the series. I thought it was spam. Turns out, it wasn't. After debating whether or not I wanted to be in a televised singing competition, I felt this opportunity must have been put in my path for a reason. The challenge was mentally preparing to head to L.A. With no official place to call home, I spent the weeks leading up to my audition packing up my things, moving them into storage and sleeping on any sofa available, in hopes that something would come of this next venture. *This is when I decided if this didn't work, I would have to give in to quitting, which I dreaded.*

> ***"To me it was never a competition against other contestants, it was more of a competition against me and my own inner demons telling me I couldn't do this"***

When I arrived in L.A, I began questioning everything about myself. Was this how I wanted to further my career? Was I cheating the system? But with much soul searching, I decided that finding the best way to achieve your goals is not cheating, it's changing your way of doing things and thinking outside of the box. If this was the opportunity that was being laid out before me, then I was going to do my best, no matter what the outcome. During one of the many vetting interviews, **I was told by one of the producers that I was "positive to a fault".** That was funny to me because little did they know the internal battle going on inside me. No matter what, I couldn't let anyone else know how distraught I was because I knew positive affirmation was the only way I was going to move ahead.

With my mind focused on doing *"my very best"*, I flew through the audition process, landed on Blake Shelton's team and was paired up for my first battle. I knew this was a contest against other people on the show with the object being to beat the other artists… but to me it was never a competition against the others. It was more of a fight with myself and my own inner demons telling me I couldn't do this. When the first battle was over, I stood in front of my coach and was not chosen to move on. Rejection is not fun for anyone, especially when it's nationally televised, but I looked inward and knew I'd done my best. As I was about to walk off the stage, knowing if this was the end of the road for me, then I could accept it and move on to that next chapter of my life, the lights flashed, buzzers went off and I was saved by Gwen Stefani, another coach on The Voice. Relief flowed through me as I realized I'd been given another chance to prove I belonged there.

They say, "If you wanna hear God laugh, tell him your plan"! Apparently going home was NOT on HIS agenda. The following week, I was put up against another artist on Team Gwen. I was once again defeated in the 2nd battle and about to step off the stage when the lights went off, the buzzer sounded, and Blake Shelton was stealing me back to his team! I can't explain the rush of emotion I felt in those 30 seconds between being rejected by Gwen and then saved again by Blake, but if I had to try, it would be like falling off a cliff and right before you hit the dirt, something swoops in and catches you. You don't know if you're crying because you're still reeling from the fear of falling or the relief of being saved.

> Reflecting back, connecting the dots, it was the same thing that had been going on in my life prior to the show. Only this time it was on television in front of millions of people, in a shorter amount of time, but with the same outcomes. I was denied, then saved, denied and saved again. The challenge ahead would not just be to prove myself to my coach, but to the voting public.... Little did I know that I already had.

As the show went "Live" and the viewers were able to decide my fate, I pushed on as I always did. Keeping faith in myself that I was doing the right thing from week to week. The struggle wasn't in the choice of songs or how I would perform them, that part was easy because I'd been doing that for 10 years prior. It was in the seconds before my name was called to stay, wondering if America understood me or if they would decide I fell short of their expectations. The fans never disappointed, they never wavered. So, as true as they were to me, I stayed true to myself. Time after time I challenged myself, never to focus on the other contestant's song choices or if I could beat them. I made many friends, offered advice to whomever asked and helped them out in their performances. I knew the outcome would be whatever was meant to be.

The weeks flew by and I found myself at the moment of truth. It was down to the final Top 4. As I was walking though set, someone yelled "Hey! There's Craig Wayne Boyd!" and without thinking, I responded *"Yep! I'm Still Here"!*

> *In that moment it hit me. All my life I lived in that moment of the song, "I Ain't No Quitter" I'd released to radio all those years back and now I was living its sequel. Never giving up, never giving in to those demons that constantly nagged at my subconscious telling me I couldn't do it and I knew I needed to write that song. I took pen to paper and began writing.*

Those who know my story and those that watched Season 7 of NBC's The Voice know the outcome but to touch briefly on that moment; I remember being on the stage with the last 4 contestants. I was the only member left from Team Blake and the other 3 were from Team Adam. We huddled together on the stage in front of a live audience as the results slowly dwindled our numbers from four to two. I watched Damien walk off first, then Chris, wondering how it was possible that I would be left to stand alone with Matt. Once again would my hopes be dashed? I'd never set out to win the show, I had come here to prove to myself that I could stand with the best and that I was worthy of being here. There I was, in the final moments, suddenly I wanted it so badly. Although I could accept second place…would this be the moment I was triumphant? Or would it turn out like every other time, where I reached up, and could feel my dreams within my grasp only to have them slip through my fingers? Would I have to "tuck my tail" and run back to Nashville to start all over? Would I have to take another career path to support my son? Where would I live? If things had gone differently, my guess is that because of my determination, I would have found a way to stay with music in some form or fashion. That's the way I was taught. It was bred in me to be that "nose to the grindstone" type of guy, and I knew I still had more fight in me.

Call it luck, call it fate, call it divine intervention, but as it turned out, I didn't have to worry about any of those questions. My name was called, and I was crowned the winner of season 7 of The Voice. In that moment of realization, I thought back to Bob Spears and his wise words for me when I was 17:

> *Each point in my life when my dreams were shattered, I pulled some knowledge from his statement as I would pick myself back up and moved forward. Each challenge, each disappointment, each victory was a tidbit I kept with me and learned from to make the next moment better. I never realized how powerful his words were until then. I knew as I held the trophy in my hand, confetti falling around me and tears in my eyes, I had conquered a mountain by simply believing in myself... and so begins a grand new journey and next chapter of my life. What will it hold?*

I'm Still Here

Written By:

Craig Wayne Boyd, Arlis Albritton & Josh Helms

I'm a believer, but there's a song in me that's begging to be heard

Yes, I'm a dreamer, hanging on to hope for everything its worth

So I skipped a few meals and slept in my car

When you're down that low they don't care who you are

In this who-do-ya-know town

Oh but look at me now

I'm still here

Standing strong

I'm Still Here

Giving it my all

Cause that's just who I am

I won't give up

I don't know what that means

It's not inside of me

To pack my bags and turn my back

Walk away just like that and disappear

I'm still here

I'm no leaver, but I gotta be where the marquee holds my name

Because I'm a singer, so I move town to town and stage to stage

But my sons at home and he's too young to know, why sometimes daddies have to go

So I point to his heart and say, son, if you ever need me, right here's where I'll be

I'm still here

Standing strong

Giving it my all

Cause that's just who I am

I won't give up

I don't know what that means

It's not inside of me

To pack my bags and turn my back

Walk away just like that and disappear

I'm still here

No, I won't give up

I don't know what that means

It's not inside of me

To pack my bags and turn my back

Walk away just like that and disappear

I'm still here

I'm still here

I'm still here

***

To contact Craig:

Website: http://www.craigwayneboyd.com

Facebook: https://www.facebook.com/Craigwayneboyd

Twitter: https://www.twitter.com/cwbyall

Instagram: https://www.instagram.com/cwbyall

Snapchat: Cwbyall

YouTube: https://www.youtube.com/Craigwayneboyd

Anoush Khaze

Anoush Khaze' is a Transformational Speaker, a Resilience Coach and a published Author who specializes in working with entrepreneurs and those who want to, overcome obstacles and challenges, but need the support, structure, inspiration, and motivation to get unstuck, Bounce Back and pursue their goals and dreams. His expertise in personal and business resilience comes from facing and overcoming a combination of both personal and professional challenges and experiences of nearly four decades in the fields of finance, information design, business development, and network marketing.

Anoush is a first-generation immigrant with an Armenian and Russian heritage who came to the U.S. at age 16. After college he worked in many sectors of the corporate world. He spent nearly a decade working in the financial industry with some of the biggest firms in the industry, where some of his past clients are among the fortune 500 companies. He has also spent over twenty years developing successful businesses.

Nurture Your Mind to Cultivate Success

Anoush Khaze

"He who has a WHY to live can bear almost any how." ~ Friedrich Nietzsche

To cultivate success, you must first nurture your mind for a success mindset. A success mindset is one that leads you toward success. Every endeavour in life should be approached as a success in the making. Instead of focusing on success itself, it is the daily objectives that help build a success mindset—daily objectives in your health and fitness goals, career endeavours, or even academic pursuits. To develop such a mindset, we must change. Changing not only the way we think, but also the way we act and respond to events in our daily lives. Change is not easy. We often resist change because we have become accustomed to the way we do things and to the way we live our lives. Changing is hard, especially if we are in our comfort zone. But we must become open and willing to change because change is at the core of our existence. Change is not only at the core of everything in life but also at the core of the universe. Everything is consistently and constantly changing. Seeds change and grow to become mighty trees; children change and grow to become adults. Astronomers tell us that even the universe has been changing throughout billions of years; it has been expanding and contracting. Even though change may be hard and uncomfortable, we must become comfortable with the uncomfortable, so we may nurture our minds and cultivate a success mindset.

To cultivate success, you must first cultivate your own mind so that it leads you toward success. It isn't about succeeding all at once, but rather taking small steps everyday towards improving yourself for the sake of discovering what each day can bring. Successes are often measurable by how we feel inside and out, not only within our lives but also our careers. This is shown through hard work combined with consistency, and most importantly, the results we accomplish.

We must focus on cultivating success in all areas of our lives, not just one, or two. From my own recent experience, it can be so easy to be focused on one or two areas of life that we end up neglecting other areas to our own detriment. How? Let me tell you a little about my experience.

Over the past decade, I have been focused on having a success mindset in accomplishing a few goals. First, it was my goal as a caregiver for my disabled wife, my 100-year-old mother, and caring and nurturing my 17-year-old son. My second goal was in regards to my career path. I wanted to build a successful resilience coaching and speaking practice and a consulting business. As well as become a published author so that I could impact the world.

In focusing on these goals, I totally neglected my own health and fitness goals and let them slide. I gained thirteen pounds that I had lost. A little over a year ago on Sunday, August 8, 2021, I found myself feeling pain in my back which then radiated to my chest. My blood pressure shot up to 190/99 and I felt like there was an elephant sitting on my chest. My son drove me to the emergency room. While I was there, I began to feel the pain radiating to my left arm and I knew what was happening. This was no doubt the sign of a massive HEART ATTACK. I told the admitting nurse how I felt and after an EKG, within 40 minutes, I found myself on the operating table due to a 100% blockage of my Left Anterior Descending Artery (LAD) nicknamed THE WIDOW MAKER. A stent was inserted to restore the flow of blood to my heart. I owe my life not just to the surgical team, but also to the E.R Doctor who diagnosed my condition, and all the nurses who did an amazing job in keeping this old boy alive.

Two days later they inserted two more stents in two arteries, with 80% and 60% blockages. Today I am fully recovered with a new lease on life, and a much clearer vision of my future. I can tell you there is nothing quite like a brush with death to give one clarity and focus on what is important.

I now realized I had to make changes in my life. I always knew that I should probably eat healthier and avoid all the oil-rich Armenian and Middle Eastern foods, and that I should exercise more. However, I was not focused on my diet, so I kept on doing what I was doing. The changes required were not easy. To be honest, eating healthy after years of not doing it is hard. I didn't like hard, and after all, who does? Change takes time and effort, and we all want things to be easy and fast. That is why we microwave the food instead of steam cooking it. I had to change not just the way I ate, exercised and lived, but I had to change my focus. I had to readjust my mindset.

Mind you, during this whole ordeal, my mindset was not that of a defeatist. Was I scared? You bet! However, I was joking and talking with the medical staff and was confident not only in their abilities, but also in the fact that I would make it through the surgery just fine because my faith would carry me.

On the battlefield of life, we face battles every day in one form or another. I believe that 99% of these battles are fought, won, or lost, first on the battlefield of our minds, before they even begin in a real-life setting. What we believe in our minds becomes our reality. We manifest our own futures with our thinking and with our mindset.

So, how exactly do you nurture your mind and cultivate a success mindset? What changes must you go through to develop this mindset? Can your mindset be cultivated, or is it just what it is? Of course, it can. Imagine for a moment planting the seed for a Chinese Bamboo tree. How would you start cultivating this tree? After planting the seed, you cover it with compost and water the seed daily. You must watch over it. Birds and squirrels will dig it up and eat it if you do not. You must nurture the seed until it germinates. While you water it and take care of it, the seed is changing, growing, slowly but steadily. The remarkable thing about this tree is that it takes five years for it to emerge from the ground. But when it sprouts, it grows rapidly in five weeks, to a height of over 80 feet – if the tree was well nurtured and cultivated correctly. Now, did it take the tree 5 years to grow to 80 feet or 5 weeks?

Nurturing a mind to cultivate a mindset for success is no different than doing so for a Chinese Bamboo tree seed. Sometimes it may take a while before the changes take effect, and you see actual results, hopefully not 5 years, but you will see the results. Nurturing anything, including our minds, is a day-by-day process. A success mindset is cultivated the same way. That is, through setting manageable goals and treating each opportunity as a chance at success and as an opportunity to change for the better, instead of seeing it as an obstacle to reaching a distant goal. Success requires work every day with no leniency. Sometimes this process takes longer for one person than for another. Some people may need to change more than others depending on their past and upbringing.

Many people have this false perception that success is based on luck and that is why on average nearly 68% of the United States population buy lottery tickets. But success is just like a seed, and our mindset towards being successful can be nurtured with the right tools. When it comes down to pursuing success, having an optimistic attitude about life, as well as improving yourself daily can be very effective tools. Once you have cultivated your mindset for success in one area, cultivating it for success in other areas of your life becomes significantly easier.

If nurturing a success mindset is the first step to cultivating success, then success strategy is its cousin and best friend. Success strategy focuses on visualization; it's the most important part of success strategies. If you can't visualize yourself succeeding at some endeavour, then you won't be able to cultivate a success mindset toward that endeavour. It takes discipline and effort to constantly see success, even when all indications point toward failure.

My mentor Dexter Yager used to say,

"If Your Dream is Big Enough, Facts Don't Count."

After visualizing your success each day, commit to following a plan of action with small daily objectives that work toward your vision of success. The power of success mindset and success strategies, if ingrained in you enough to be supportive tools for success rather than just words on a page, will push you forward towards your goal.

Next, you want to shift your mindset so that nothing is getting in your way. In doing so, keep in mind that there are many different mindsets one can cultivate toward success. I am going to focus on just a couple of them.

There are many different types of success, but they aren't all equal when it comes to mindset. Some mindsets will serve you better than others depending on what kind of work you do and how much support you have from family and friends along the way. It also depends on what success means to you. Success may mean landing an interview for a job you want— or getting a promotion; or it may mean making money by starting and sustaining your own business. Whatever it is, success is the end result, the goal.

Sometimes you must fight daily to maintain and develop your mindset for success. So, you must be flexible, be willing and able to change and adapt. Therefore, I will start with the adaptability mindset because this one is often overlooked, but in my personal experience it is incredibly important. No matter what success you achieve, there is always a chance that you will hit a roadblock somewhere along the line and realize that success does not taste so sweet anymore. If your success was due to a specific situation (like success at a certain job) or outside circumstances (like having great family support), then yes—you will continue to succeed for as long as these characteristics remain constant. But for most people, success comes from hard work and determination—and if either of these things change (or even completely disappear), then so will success, at least for a brief time, while you bounce back and find a different approach. This requires a mindset for Resilience.

Resilience mindset is also crucial, because when the pursuit of success gets tough, most people give up without allowing themselves any time to recharge their batteries and instead start considering other ways to succeed. If you are going to rely on any two mindsets for success, Adaptability and Resilience should be the ones you consider. Success does not usually happen right away, and it comes along with its fair share of difficulties.

My mentor Dexter Yager used to say,

"You have to give yourself time to succeed."

It is essential that you nurture your mind to have a mindset geared toward success if you want to succeed in general. Every successful person had obstacles placed in their path at one point or another (these are the biggest success killers) but rather than giving up (Resilience), they adjusted their plans (Adaptability) and moved forward by working around those issues.

My mentor Jim Agard used to say,

"Put Your Plans in Sand, and Your Dreams in Concrete."

One thing that I always ask my clients is *"Are you a Rubber Ball or a Bean Bag?"*

When life knocks you down, do you just lay there like a Bean Bag, complain and whine; or do you bounce back like a Rubber Ball? Bouncing back and picking yourself up after a setback is crucial not only because success won't come right away but also because if a roadblock stops you from pressing forward towards your goal, then it will likely be difficult to get back up and start again.

When you make changes and nurture your mind to develop success habits, you will be more likely to achieve success. Success is all about the small steps you take forward every day. Cultivating success habits leads to success on a larger scale as those practices become consistent in your life.

When I was going to school in Iran, we learned how to do electrical wiring for a house in our shop class. I came to the United States when I was 16 years old. One day when I was visiting my uncle, who knew I had learned electrical wiring in Iran, he asked me if I could do the wiring for his attic, which he was converting into an apartment. Although I had the knowledge and the skill, I had never wired an entire apartment before, but I accepted the job because my uncle was paying $500, which was a lot of money back then. I also only had 3 weeks to complete the job.

First, I went to the library and looked up the state electrical codes to learn the requirements and made a list of the necessary supplies. Then I went with my uncle to the hardware store to get what we needed. Every day after school and on the weekends, I went to his house and worked on the wiring. I finished the project within the 3-week time limit, and it passed the city inspection.

So, what is the point of this story? I was only a teenager, with no experience, but I knew that *Given the Necessary Time and Resources, There Was Nothing I Could Not Do*. It all goes back to a mindset nurtured for success. It is all about your self-belief. It is all about your self-image.

You may be thinking, "Well goodie for you Anoush, you can do it; you have the right mindset. What about me? How am I going to do it?" Here is the good news. If I can do it, you can too. I am not an anomaly. I am not some magical being that can accomplish anything that I set my mind to. Many times, I faced failures and challenges. The reason I was able to overcome those challenges and failures was because I was willing to change and to learn. Over the years I changed and learned to look at failures and obstacles from a different perspective. I learned to look at failures as lessons of what not to do, and I look at obstacles as challenges to overcome, which is a Resilience Mindset.

This did not happen overnight. It was the result of associating with the right people, reading the right books, listening to the right audios, and being mentored by people far more successful than myself in the areas that I was trying to become successful in.

Am I saying that I had more than one mentor? Yes, exactly! You may need a mentor for success in your job and another if you are building a side business. You will also need another mentor if you are trying to become a millionaire, or a billionaire and you need to follow their guidance and advice. I remember once I was debating with my mentor Jim Agard about a point where I thought I was right. He asked me a simple question; *"Do you want to be right, or do you want to be rich?"* I got the point; he had the fruit on the tree. He was already a multimillionaire, and for me to argue about a point in an area where he had already proven himself was foolish.

In the end I will leave you with these three points which are from my own experiences and what I have learned from my mentors on how to cultivate your mindset for success. The ground on which you plant the seed of success mindset must be fertile. It means you must be receptive, open-minded, and realize that you do not have all the answers. You must be teachable and coachable to succeed.

You must nourish the seed of success mindset with the right nourishments daily. It means that you will have to invest in yourself like you did with buying this book. Make sure you are reading the right books, watching positive videos or shows, and listening to the positive podcasts and audios. Forget Netflix[1], ABC[1], CBS[1], NBC[1], CNN[1] and all those other channels that do nothing for you but consume your most precious commodity, your *"TIME."* Instead subscribe to services like Audible[1], Mentor Box[1], Wondrium[1] and Master Class[1].

Be very critical about who you associate with. Associate with only people at your level and up; people who are at your level of ambition and success or higher. Confucius, a Chinese philosopher, who lived way before the sixth century BC, wrote one of his many quotes about surrounding yourself with good people. *"If you are in any room and think that you're the smartest person there then I'm sorry to inform you but they have wronged their guest."*

Cultivating your mindset for success is a daily endeavour, but one that pays off in dividends. Changing just one thing about the way you think could be all it takes to reach new heights of productivity and happiness. Pursue this goal with diligence and dedication and see where you can go!

***

To contact Anoush:

http://www.AnoushKhaze360.com

1) Netflix[1], ABC[1], CBS[1], NBC[1], CNN[1], Audible[1], Mentor Box[1], Wondrium[1] and Master Class[1] are the trademarks of their respective companies.

Jennifer Pilates

"Empowering and Transforming Body, Mind & Spirits Worldwide for 20+Yrs" – Jennifer Pilates

Jennifer Pilates has been transforming clients' bodies, minds, and spirits worldwide for over 20 years as a Celebrity Trainer and Empowerment Mindset Coach, Host of the Top-Rated Podcast: Empowered Within, and internationally renowned Intuitive Advisor. Jennifer is a multi-passionate entrepreneur, detail-loving, stubborn-as-heck achiever, unshakeable optimist, self-care activist, fur-baby momma, and ocean-loving intuitive empath.

"I started my Pilates practice over 20 years ago after being in a traumatic car accident. I had no idea that my Pilates rehabilitative program would not only change me physically but also alter the direction of my life. Through Pilates, I was guided to a deeper understanding of the Body, Mind & Spirit which enhanced my spiritual gifts and elevated my abilities as an intuitive empath. – Jennifer Pilates

From her coaching to training, from her advising to her top-rated Podcast: Empowered Within, Jennifer has been leaving her inspirational, empowering, and transformational touch on clients and celebrities worldwide for over two decades!

"My goal is to help you discover your own truths, gain self-empowerment and in turn transform Body, Mind and Spirit." – Jennifer

How to Live an Empowered Life from Within

By Jennifer Pilates

"I started my Pilates practice over 20 years ago after being in a traumatic car accident. I had no idea that my Pilates rehabilitative program would not only change me physically but also alter the direction of my life. Through Pilates, I was guided to a deeper understanding of the Body, Mind & Spirit which enhanced my spiritual gifts and elevated my abilities as an intuitive empath." – Jennifer Pilates

Over the years, I have learned that to live an empowered life within is a choice. It doesn't come in a moment but in a lifetime of experiences, from happiness to sadness, from loves and losses to journeys and great adventures. Living an empowered life from within is learning to live from an empowered place within yourself where every step is aligned with your heart's desires, being in the moment, not projecting into the future, and not wallowing in the past. It's just that moment. Building moment upon moment is how we get to that place of feeling aligned and empowered within body, mind, and spirit.

For me, learning to live an empowered life from within began after a traumatic car accident. I was driving home from work at a red light; I looked up and saw a car speeding toward me. I looked to my right, and my left and I knew that there was nowhere for me to go. The car hit me, I ping-ponged back-and-forth, and I must've had a moment or two of unconsciousness. It was at that moment that the trajectory of my life was forever changed.

Before the accident, I was climbing the corporate ladder in the senior living industry specializing in Alzheimer's disease. I started in the industry when I was fifteen and worked my way up from the kitchen to the top. But, in retrospect, everything I loved about the industry, being an advocate for and all the interaction with the residents and their families, I was pulled away from as I climbed further up the ladder. It was now all numbers and budgets. Everything that I loved about the industry I was no longer in flow with; I was miserable.

"Life doesn't happen to you; it happens for you." – Tony Robbins

Like my traumatic car accident, it is in these pivotal moments when the greatest, most monumental, amazing things happen in our lives. In these moments, there is a lesson and a blessing. It's about mindset, shifting from "why is this happening to me?" to "how is this happening for me?" When we're in the thick of it, we don't always see it, nor does it always feel like it. However, if we take a moment to step back, we can get there. What I learned from my traumatic car accident was priceless. It was the most amazing blessing in disguise.

Everything changed; I could no longer do the job, I could no longer drive to work, and I could no longer be the person that I was. I was evolving I was someone with trauma and soft tissue damage from the base of my skull down through the base of my spine. I was evolving as I was in and out of doctors' offices for 7-8 hours a day— a combination of chiropractors, massage therapists, acupuncturists, psychologists, and neurologists for months. I was re-learning vocabulary and learning how intricately the mind and body worked together.

I was in the mecca of the wellness community in Boulder, Colorado, which was an incredible blessing. I could experience modalities I had never heard of before and wouldn't have otherwise experienced. I was referred to a fantastic woman who specialized in rehabilitative care who, no coincidence, happened to be a Pilates trainer. I learned the intricacies of the body, mind, and spirit connection from her. Through my Pilates rehabilitation program, I realized how interconnected and interwoven the body, mind, and spirit are. I also learned how incredibly amazing it feels when we are in alignment. It's not easy, and we're only sometimes going to stay in it. After all, we are perfectly imperfect human beings, each and every one of us. However, once you get a feel of it, I can promise you will fight for that empowering body, mind, and spirit alignment, that transformation that you can feel, that empowering feeling within.

Through the Pilates rehabilitative program, my life was truly changed forever. I learned so much about myself through that program that I didn't know. I learned that before the accident, I was doing what I knew, what I saw, what I grew up with, and what society expected of me. Now I was learning what I wanted to do, what lit me up and brought out passion from within me. I became empowered within, and it was during that year that everything changed for me. Through the car settlement, I had just enough money to go to the Pilates Center, the Harvard of all Pilates training centers. Again, no coincidence it was right there in Boulder, CO. The universe has a unique way of lining things up for us.

"We grow through what we go through." – Jennifer Pilates

As for my corporate career, I knew there would be layoffs, so I offered to be laid off. At the time, I was only in my late 20s, and all I had known was working in the senior living industry, in assisted living communities, and specializing in Alzheimer's disease. I didn't understand the impact of what I was saying when I said, "lay me off if need be." So, I made this huge decision, not even understanding all the consequences. However, looking back, I was going with the flow. I was beginning to flow with my life versus swimming upstream, living unhappily. It was in those moments that I found myself, even in those moments where I felt the most unsure about everything. I was walking away from a career; from everything I was supposed to be doing and interning. Instead, I found everything that I loved, and I found my empowered self.

My intuitive empath abilities heightened through my Pilates rehabilitative program and training. In retrospect, I knew in those moments that this was an incredible opportunity to be a holistic practitioner to bring healing and to help empower others.

I always felt throughout my Pilates training program that my mission was that if I could help one person not to be in pain, just one, it would mean the world to me. When I found Pilates, I had been in so much pain, unsure, and insecure about everything. I was a caterpillar in a cocoon; I couldn't see in the dark. Pilates shined a light and guided me through my healing journey onto a path of awakening and healing. Awakening to self, awakening into feeling empowered within my body, and understanding the genuine connection between my body, mind, and spirit.

My mission when I graduated from The Pilates Center School was to help one person not be in pain. I would be satisfied if I could help one person not to feel what I had to feel. Now, 20+ years later, I've had the honor of serving thousands and thousands of celebrities, professional athletes, and those recovering from injuries from ages

8-88 worldwide on their healing journey, transforming and empowering body, mind, and spirit.

My Pilates practice led me down the path of becoming a holistic practitioner. I have expanded my Pilates practice to offer empowering mindset coaching where I combine all my modalities as an intuitive empath, helping clients find their empowering place within. I used to say that being an intuitive empath was a blessing and a curse. Having healed and evolved by employing my healing tools, it's an incredible blessing. It's my superpower. It's a blessing and an honor to share all I have learned and experienced over the years and serve many people worldwide. To encompass a genuine body, mind, and spirit practice for my clients is a dream come true.

Being able to help and serve was a mission of mine long before I ever knew that was my mission. When I look back throughout my life, starting at 15 years old in the retirement industry, and all of the seniors and their families that I was able to help, learning how to be an advocate for self, and assisting others in advocating for themselves was so fulfilling. To be able to take all of the modalities that I have learned over the years and bring that into one practice to help and serve clients worldwide is an incredible blessing.

How Do You Learn to Live an Empowered Life from Within?

It's about stepping back, stepping out of the emotions, and looking at the bird's eye view of everything that's going on in your life and knowing that in a single moment, everything can change and that you can make that change. You have the power to make that shift in mindset. All you have to do is decide. Once you are aligned, and everything comes together, nothing can stop you. Yes, there are trials and tribulations in life. But, of course, that is the adventure, the journey, and the school of life. We are here to learn. You always have the power to return to self and shift your mindset. You always have the choice to come from an empowered place. That's how I work with and guide clients, bringing them back to self and shining a light where mindset shifts are possible, whether that is personally or professionally. Whatever challenges or patterns are playing out at work are most likely playing out at home, with friends and family, and vice versa. Once you determine the challenges or patterns, you can go to the root of the emotions and triggers, and you have the power to release the limiting beliefs through.

"There is a lesson and a blessing in every situation." – Jennifer Pilates

You also have the opportunity to see the blessing in the situation, although it can be challenging. However, the blessings are there when we choose to know that we have the power; we have that power to sit in sadness for hours and hours, or we can choose to allow ourselves to feel our emotions and allow them to pass through us. Emotions are not meant to stagnate you. They are meant to pass through you, and you are meant to learn from them. You are becoming empowered by them as you allow them to pass through and release them. That is an incredibly empowering place to get to once you realize that you are meant to live from an empowered place you create from within yourself.

I started working with a client who came to me feeling lost. She did not feel she had a voice and did not feel worthy of her dreams. We customized a coaching program for her around the triggers and challenges she was facing both at home and work. Here is what she has to say about her time working with me: "Jennifer, I just wanted to say thank you for all that you have done for me. When we met you, I was lost but with your help, you showed me that I had a voice, that I mattered, my dreams mattered. Thank you - words can't express how grateful I am for you." – LM

There is another client of mine that I have been working with for ten years. When we started, our work was centered around her feeling less than in her career and personal life. After digging deep, we began working through childhood triggers, noticing patterns in her day-to-day life. By being able to dig deep, she shifted her mindset, released her limiting beliefs, removed her people-pleasing thoughts, and began living from an empowered place within. She began living for her. Here is what she has to say about her time working with me: "You always give me the best guidance. I'm so grateful to you, even when it's hard to hear. For ten years, Jennifer, you have always been right. That is amazing. Cheers to his next part, it's going to be amazing, thank you." SP

I practice what I preach. I continue to work on myself in my new journey and adventure. The more I work on myself and continue to heal, the more I can help and serve others. That is ultimately the mission; to continue to help, serve, and bring forth empowerment to you.

So, I ask, "Are you ready to live an empowered life from within? Are you ready to align your body, mind, and spirit? Are you ready to live the life of your dreams from an empowered place? It is within those moments when you say yes-yes-yes, I am ready. I am worthy. I deserve it. I have so much to give to this world. I love myself. I believe in myself. I am open to creative possibilities. I am ready. It is in those moments that the magic happens. It is in those moments that you find your empowered self from within.

My challenge for you now is to grab a journal and write down your dreams and aspirations. Stretch your mind. Not looking at your life, I want you to go within and feel the life you know you deserve. Please write that out. When you write something down, it is so compelling. You are genuinely putting it out there for the universe. I am worthy of my dream house. I am desirable. I am prosperous. I am financially free. I am beautiful. I am creative. Write it all out. Take five minutes a day and begin to do this, and I can promise you that your life will start to change. Your energies are changing. Your vibration is changing. You are attracting a higher vibration, and you're attracting your dreams, the people, and the places that will help you to get there. All you have to do is shift your mindset. All you have to do is say yes! I am ready to live the life of my dreams. Yes, I am ready to live an empowered life from within.

Remember my journey. It didn't happen over one night. I ultimately evolved from my car accident into being a rehabilitative Pilates trainer and Empowerment Mindset Coach who has worked with celebrities, corporate executives, and amazing people from around the world for over 20+ years. My intuitive empath abilities are enhanced, allowing me to feel what you're going through. I am on this journey with you. I see it and feel it all, so you show up as yourself, as your perfectly imperfect self, and we will work with your mindset, emotions, triggers, and everything that has been holding you back from living an empowered life from within.

I am empowering myself daily in nature, within the world around me, and moving forward into the unknown. There are so many things that I don't know at this moment. I could focus on the insecurities and the fears, or I could shift my mindset and empower myself by helping and serving others. I can continue to show up to the world each day to my best ability.

This has been an incredibly empowering experience. Once I could take a step back and shift my mindset, I realized there were a lot of lessons I could learn. There are also a lot of blessings that have come forth. It takes time, and it is essential to have grace with yourself, love yourself, and know when to just be.

We are all collectively at an incredibly pivotal moment in life worldwide. We are being asked to wake up to what aligns with our body, mind, and spirit. Wake up to finding gratitude in day-to-day life, finding the blessings and the life lessons. That, my friend, is when you are aligning and flowing. Then, you can embrace, learn to grow, and feel empowered within.

The only limitations that we put on ourselves are our own limiting beliefs. When we shift our mindset and are ready to say "enough," we can soar to new heights. I hope you find this inspiring, motivational, and above all else, empowering. I hope you have found moments where you have felt empowered to take a step forward. One step is all you need. It is up to you, my friend. So, I say again, are you ready to live an empowered life from within?

I know that you are, and I know that you have it in you, and when you are ready, I am here for you. I would love and be honored to continue this conversation when you are ready. It would be my honor to help guide you to that place of truly living an empowered life from within.

"My mission is to help clients discover their own truths, gain self-empowerment and in turn transform their lives, Body, Mind, and Spirit." – Jennifer Pilates

***

To contact Jennifer:

Email: Info@JenniferPilates.com

Book a Consultation: https://jenniferpilates.com/

Facebook: https://www.facebook.com/JenniferPliates

Instagram: https://www.instagram.com/thejenniferpilates/

YouTube: https://www.youtube.com/channel/UCkhV033DQEauG2X9AKs7mLA

Pinterest: htttps://www.pinterest.com/TheJenniferPilates/

Rich Steffen

Rich Steffen is a business and life success coach, personal development trainer, and speaker. He holds his Life Mastery Consultant Certification and is a Certified Master Practitioner in neuro-linguistic programming. Rich has been coaching business owners and individuals since 2014.

Over the course of Rich's 43-year career, he has embodied various roles in 6 different businesses ranging from restaurants to real estate, with coaching being the seventh. Each position contributes a puzzle piece to the diversity of experience that Rich resources today in his style and strategies as a business and life success coach.

He has developed two programs, Engage Your Genius and Mindset Matrix, both encompassing common principles of success that have resulted from his love of personal development, countless hours of education, and a passion for seeing others achieve milestones of success in their lives they never thought possible.

Rich refers to coaching as his "End Game" and his other business ventures as the steppingstones that have provided him with the same clarity of purpose, he desires to empower his clients. Rich is an empowering and engaging coach that routinely offers to "Get in the Weeds" with his clients, AKA his community.

When not working with his community, Rich enjoys hiking, photography, horseback riding, and time with family.

Creating A Successful Personal Structure

By Rich Steffen

Growing up and until age 35, if someone asked me if I had a Successful Personal Structure, I would have responded with a confident "Yes, I do!"

I was blessed with great parents that gave me the support and permission to experience many terrific opportunities as I grew up and before I moved out on my own. From a young age, I had awesome friends, was a very adventurous Boy Scout troop member, and worked on my grandfather's ranch, baling hay, and branding cattle. I spent my three high school summers working at a dude ranch in Colorado, leading guided tours through the Rocky Mountain National Park on horseback, climbed my first "14'er," and started my first small business selling items I pulled out of the K-Mart dumpsters that customers had returned; to name a few because there were many more.

After graduating from high school, I moved to Colorado to live in the mountains for a year with a friend I worked with at the dude ranch. We did work while there, but only enough to pay the bills. So, my friend and I spent the rest of our time trying to squeeze in as many great experiences as possible! In the warmer months, we hiked, backpacked, and did our fair share of technical rock climbing. In the winter, it was skiing and snowshoeing. Finally, after successfully maximizing all 12 months, we both moved back home.

Once back, I got another restaurant job and moved into an apartment with two of my co-workers. Then one night after work, one of my roomies tossed out the idea that since none of us had ever seen the ocean before, we should take a trip to San Diego. So, we were packed in the car three hours later and drove to California. Before our two-week visit ended, we rented a house because we were moving to San Diego! San Diego was home for the next three years, and for the duration of my time there, I had the opportunity to work in one of San Diego's most popular restaurants, an experience that provided a significant pivot point for me.

Cleverly Disguised Opportunity

About a year had gone by when one day, the general manager pulled me aside and shared with me that the kitchen manager had been diagnosed with a terminal disease, was not returning to work, and asked if I would be willing to assume his position. Of course, I agreed and did that successfully for the next two years. Toward the end of my time there, the general manager pulled me aside and asked if I had ever considered applying for an actual management position with the company. He went on to say that the director of H.R. would be in town to interview another applicant, and he could set it up for me to interview as well. I told him I had not ever thought about it, but sure!

It was the day of the interview, and while waiting for the director to arrive, I had a chance to talk with the other applicant. The only thing he said that caught my attention was that he had just gotten his degree and had no restaurant experience. I remember silently saying to myself, "this will be a cakewalk!" However, upon arriving for work the following day, I was informed that the other applicant was awarded the position, and the reason given was, "you did not have a college degree." That knocked me back on my heels. It was the only time I could remember when working hard did not win the day, which was a very tough pill to swallow.

Then, one warm February day, I was in San Diego. I received a call from the restaurant company's home office, and it was the corporate chef. He told me his dad was on the Culinary Institute of America board in New York and thought this would be an excellent fit for me. He said there was an 18-month waitlist, but his dad could get me in as soon as I could make it happen. That call quickly removed "the burn" I was experiencing from my interview, and two months later, I was in class at the C.I.A. Over the next three and a half years, I acquired my culinary and restaurant management degrees, met the woman I would marry, and moved back to California to start this career.

On the Red Carpet

Once in California, I hired on with a restaurant group and worked for them for the next nine years. I was 26 years old. What I experienced in those nine years went way, and I mean way, beyond my expectations. I started as a kitchen manager, and within four years, I was a regional manager for the western third of the U.S. This included the opportunity to oversee the corporate management training facility and the corporate test kitchen. I had a company car, a generous monthly budget to check out the food of "the competition," and the opportunity to rub elbows with some of the biggest-name chefs in the industry. What I was hired to do seemed to come so naturally to me that I could not believe they paid me to do it! I had the motivation to hit the floor running every day and was rejuvenated by a job that chewed most people up and spit them out.

God Sends a Teacher

One day it all came to an end. I received a letter that the parent company had sold the restaurant group, and my position would be eliminated. Yes, it was unfortunate to lose a job I loved, along with all the benefits it provided, but the most regrettable loss was one I did not fully grasp until years later. The loss of a position allowed me to operate "In My Lane ." In my mind, what I lost could easily be duplicated, but give me a couple of weeks, and I'll be back in the saddle with another great job, no problem. As a result, my wife and I decided to take the opportunity to move closer to family, sell the house, and move to Kansas City.

The following 17 years consisted of 5 different jobs, and none of them came close to providing me with the "In My Lane" experience I had lost. At the beginning of each new career, life was content because it was something new, but that wore off quickly. The thought that began to surface and became more frequent was, what would life be like now that an "In My Lane" job was seemingly impossible to find? I needed to get over it, be happy having a job I like versus love, and focus on the financial opportunity. Succeeding had now turned into coping.

Coming Out of the Desert

Then one day, as I was perusing my collection of self-help books that I had accumulated over the years, I landed on one I had purchased several years prior and started reading it several times, only to put it back on the shelf. The title is "Ordering Your Private World" by Gordan McDonald. This time when I picked it up, I had a hard time putting it down. That day I realized that something needed to change. His book motivated me to reflect on my past and connect the dots. As McDonald puts it, "time for a thorough scouring of the inside of life."

The realizations that surfaced from connecting the dots that I found to be most relevant are:

I am very clear on the significance and what it feels like to be "In My Lane."

A Successful Life or Business Structure is impossible without having a Successful Personal Structure.

In every position I held, I found myself involved in a training or mentoring position, and that was a part of the job I always enjoyed.

Our past is to be viewed as our teacher and not our master.

We are born with everything we need to be successful in our lives.

It's not that others have more to offer; they are just offering more of what they have.

It was through connecting the dots that I decided to become a Business and Life Success Coach. My focus is helping others create their own Successful Personal Structure, starting with discovering and developing their most significant asset, themselves.

I now want to share with you the components of a process I have used for myself and currently with my clients, called the Four D's. The Four D's are Discover, Develop, Dedicate and Deploy. The first objective is to Discover all the facets of what it means to be you; how you are wired, your zone of genius. The second objective is to develop what you have discovered about your zone of genius to the point of being able to use it and own it. The third objective is to Dedicate what you now own to your life and business. The final aim is to Deploy or take action with a mindset of resourcefulness and gratitude.

Discover

Gifts, Skills, and Talents

Gifts are what you were born with, your God-given, innate wiring that makes you who you are. When your gifts, skills, and talents are fully understood and implemented, your competition disappears because no one will do, nor can they do, no matter how hard they try, you are as great as you! Your greatest asset in life is you, and when you are clear about who you are, you will love yourself more than you can imagine, and that is when things start to show up. It's not about whom we want to become but who we already are at our best. None of us are great at everything. We need to OWN who we are. Permit ourselves to accept our weaknesses. The old saying is, "Everyone has a dork factor. Own yours!"

Values

Values are what is important to us. Not always what we like, but always what is important to us. Values are beliefs that we hold as a result of the experiences we've had in life. Values create motivation, determine our behavior, and are essential to our personality. Our values provide us with a structure or filter for the decisions we make and actions we take. Our values are also a massive contributor to our purpose, and when we function congruently with our values, our goals are much easier to achieve. Assessments are typically used to determine a list of a person's values as well as how strong those values are.

Vision

I want to start by drawing your attention to what often gets overlooked: the distinction between a vision and a goal. Goals are finite, something we work toward, and are the markers we use to measure our achievement. Visions are infinite, something we work from, and are an invitation to what can be or happen. An analogy I like to use is that of a professional football player. Their goals are 1st downs and touchdowns. Their vision is the Super Bowl. The vision is what can happen and provides the internal motivation for all the hard work required to achieve the goals. And if you can see how you can make your vision a reality, then your vision needs to be bigger! Visions, to be effective, should be so clear that you can easily connect to them using all 5 of your senses.

Questions To Help Fully Embody Your Vision

How does your perfect day unfold?

Who is around you?

What do you see?

How do you feel?

What do you hear?

What do you smell?

What is the temperature?

How does the day end?

Questions To Help Test The Validity Of Your Vision

Does my Vision give me more life?

Does my Vision align with my values?

Does my Vision require me to grow?

Does my Vision require help from a Higher Power?

Does my Vision have good in it for others?

Develop

Once you have discovered your gifts, talents, skills, values, and vision, and with the clarity necessary to own them, the next step is to develop the combination to make them usable in your life and business. Now when I say "own," I mean that they all resonate with you undeniably and comfortably. When you can truly own what you have discovered, there is a substantially reduced risk of being distracted by alternatives like "silver bullets" or dissuaded by those in your sphere who tend to whisper opinions in your ear.

In the Develop step, we see the creation of purpose, often referred to as our WHY. This brings up another important distinction: our WHY has two sides. The first side of our WHY is the one we all recognize, which is why we do what we do. The second side of our WHY is why we do what we do...the way we do it. I like to use a simple analogy: if we were standing in the kitchen with a dirty floor, each of us would be given a mop and told to mop the floor. Will we get the floor cleaned? Yes. Will we mop the floor the same way, going the same direction, at the same speed, using the same stroke pattern? Not likely. The first WHY typically represents external motivation, and the second internal motivation. Combining the two becomes the filter for everything we think and do. Actions taken in the vein of our WHY create fulfillment. Not in our WHY allows room to be governed by our performance and not our identity. The struggles we experience in life with people and situations directly reflect how right we are with our WHY. Remember, finding our WHY is also a process of eliminating those things that are not our WHY.

When your reticular activator is on your WHY setting, here are some things you may experience:

Activities that make you come alive

Patterns and opportunities amidst complications

Things that people count on you most

Activities you do all the time and always want to know more about

Tasks that come naturally and seem like nothing special

Our WHY is an ever-evolving process. Refining your WHY is a relational, not academic, process; as a result, it will take time. The relationship is with yourself and God. The refining process includes surrounding ourselves with what I call "Partners in Believing." They fit into one of 3 categories: those that want what I have, those that want what I want, and those that have what I want. Realize that the ultimate step of refining is when your WHY is making the contribution you wish to.

Dedicate

This step is where what has been discovered and developed aligns with action. When our opportunities and actions are aligned with our vision and values and meet the F.I.T. requirements, we know those opportunities and efforts are worth our time, energy, and attention. F.I.T. stands for:

FOCUS: Is the opportunity aligned with what you are currently focused on, or is it an opportunity that will best serve you at another time?

INTENTION: Is this opportunity or action aligned with your desire to show up in the world and the value you want to contribute?

TIME: Do I want to commit the time and energy it will take to see this through?

Q: At the end of your life, what will be your greatest accomplishment if things unfold as you prefer?

Q: What do you need to change to make that a reality?

Q: If your commitment level is less than 10, what stops you from fully committing?

When operating aligned with our identity, there is a level of resiliency and peace. So do something today that your future self will thank you for. Connect based on who you are, your aspirations, and your core values. Remember, destiny is our God-given right, but along with that comes the responsibility of alignment.

Deploy

As you deploy your new Successful Personal Structure, I'd like to leave you with these to ponder:

When you take the 1st step out of your comfort zone is when creativity will flow.

Success is 10% strategy, 10% community, and 80% mindset.

When things need to be fixed, notice what you're seeing and focus on what you want.

Never forget that you always have the power to choose:

To be in a resource-full state or a resource-less state.

To respond (thought out) to a situation or to react (knee-jerk) to it.

Don't put off the benefits of being grateful until you have reached your goal – take the time to be thankful for where you are currently and for how far you've come.

As you navigate the gap between where you are now and where you want to be, know that objectivity from a trusted 3rd party will be crucial to your success.

***

To Contact Rich:

Phone: (816) 560-8494

Email: rich@richsteffen.com

LinkedIn: www.linkedin.com/in/richsteffen

Stacie Barber

Stacie Barber is a Licensed Occupational Therapist, Co-Owner of The Mindful Body Pilates Studio, Founder of Stacie Barber Coaching and is an Integrative Lifestyle + Wellness Coach working with women who are ready to unveil the truth of their inherent VALUE and WORTH and step into the next, highest version of themselves that they fully deserve. She provides authentic support and guidance through profound Guidance + Mentorship, Containers of Sisterhood, Storytelling + Inspiration, and Education + Instruction. She trusts in the power and pure resiliency of humanity and believes we are always being called into our personal version of excellence. It is her honor to support others in any capacity along their journey to self-exploration.

Taking the Leap - Leaning into Truth

By Stacie Moody-Barber

"When you walk to the edge of all the light you have and take that first step into the darkness of the unknown, you must believe that one of two things will happen. There will be something solid for you to stand upon or you will be taught to fly."---Patrick Overton

Taking the leap, learning to trust and surrender the outcome, and having the courage to look over the ledge in the first place can simultaneously feel exhilarating and frightening. When we meet the boundaries of our current circumstances and are asked to step forward and beyond, we can feel the buzz of anticipation. We can also feel stuck in our tracks. However, what I have come to know in my life is that that nudge, that deep knowing, is there to help us expand. To grow into the next version of the human and the spirit that we are meant to be. It's there to guide and direct us, to lay down the breadcrumbs to show us the way forward. Sometimes the nudge is clear, other times it can feel muted or uncertain, but it is always there. Our inner compass is a trusted companion in this journey we call life, and it has all hands-on deck to be our first mate. But first, we must realize how much we need the direction and guidance it has to offer. We must become aware of how instrumental it can be in our lives. We must lean in.

This knowing has come to me in a variety of ways and avenues in my life, some difficult and some not, but it has always come. As a child I spent many moments in a space of internal reflection and confusion. Growing up in a home with a parent that abused alcohol regularly crafted the landscape in which I quickly became aware of the leaning in. Leaning in for safety, leaning in for comfort, leaning in for solitude, leaning in for space, leaning in for peace. My outer world was not predictable; therefore, I found my internal grounding by leaning in. However, the waves and current of life can at times rock us from our safe haven and we can find ourselves miles away from ourselves and our true essence. This is my story. A story of coming back home to myself after the waves crashed down and shook the previous reality in which I had known.

During my teenage years, following my parents' tumultuous divorce, I found myself in a space of seeking outside myself. Seeking a sense of safety, love, acceptance, validation, and permission to simply BE. The external world became my compass of how to show up, be and live my life. I was more separated from my essence than I had ever been. I had allowed myself to leave myself. I abandoned who I was. I found myself involved in destructive relationships, experiencing an unplanned pregnancy, adopting disordered eating patterns, self-hate, and depression and eventually dropping out of high school. There were many days that I couldn't face myself in the mirror or even leave my house. I wasn't happy with who I had become. I was unhappy, and overall, completely disappointed in myself. Then one day, the consequences of my actions met me face to face. I didn't recognize the person I saw in the mirror and felt more lost than I had in my entire life. I had hit rock bottom. I had found a darkness that I had never known before.

"Only in the darkness can we glimpse the fullest light our soul carries for us." Angie Weiland-Crosby

In that darkness, I was forced to truly look at myself and remember who I was at my core, my soul. I was reminded of my essence, my light, and the majesty of being able to have this human experience. Those moments, in some of the darkest days of my life, I gained a knowing and deep understanding of the totality of this journey we call life. Of the incredible opportunity we have to inspire and lift up ourselves and others each and every day. But I knew it had to begin with me. I had to choose myself and my well-being over and over again. I had to learn how to deeply and unconditionally love myself. Practice forgiveness and adopt a courageousness and strength to be vulnerable and honest with myself and others. I was being asked to step back into my integrity and give myself the grace to move forward as a whole, broken human being. Through hours of meditation, quiet reflection, prayer, surrender, release, and deep forgiveness. I began recognizing myself once more.

I began to allow purpose to sprout from my pain and see the beauty in each person's experience and journey. As I met my boundaries with bravery and stepped, one foot at a time, into my next version, I was met with the humbling truth that we each have a story of our own. Shining the light on some of the most difficult moments and experiences of my life allowed others the permission to heal their own. As the wise sage Maya Angelou said, "We are more alike, my friends, than we are unalike."

"Vulnerability is not winning or losing; it's having the courage to show up and be seen when we have no control over the outcome. Vulnerability is not weakness; it's our greatest measure of courage." Brené Brown

As I continued on my path of truth, honesty, and transparency I was fully met with the calling of my life, helping others remember their greatness. Helping them uncover the light of their soul and live this life fully and purposefully. Remembering the root of who they are, who they are meant to be, and allowing their internal compass to come back online. Turning down the volume on the external to tune into their own hearts.

I am continually amazed at the impact these truths have had on the lives of those I love and cherish. Re-learning how to reconnect to their deep intuition and truth. Allowing themselves to be in a space of not knowing and trusting that the path will be shown to them. I have had the privilege to walk beside incredible humans who are taking the chance to be honest with themselves (sometimes for the first time in their lives). To shine the light on their past pain and allow their life to heal and blossom as they had never imagined possible. They are fully accepting the truth that the only way through is in. I am amazed at the transformations these practices have made in my life and the lives of others.

"There will be something solid for you to stand upon or you will be taught to fly."

When we come to the crossroads of life, will we choose a life of bravery and faith in the unwavering support around us or will we stay in a space of comfort? In my life, I have found over and over again the power of leaning in, standing in faith, and taking the leap.

Knowing that I will find something solid to stand on or I will be taught how to fly.

Why not fly?

Why not experience the amazingness of this life?

Why not live this life fully?

We only have one ticket for this ride we call life, why not take in all the bounty that it has to offer?

I have continually met this question in my life with a resounding YES and stand in awe of all that life has provided. When my father was dying from the disease that broke my childhood home, I said YES to caring for him wholeheartedly. I showed him compassion and love and forgave his impact on my life in order to fully experience mine. When I felt the nudge to resign from a career that I had built my entire adult life and family around, I said YES in order to step more fully into my purpose. To co-create a life that I couldn't yet see. When I had the opportunity to buy a business that would allow me to build something that I would be truly proud of, I said YES because I knew that I would never be in that walk alone. As I hear the voice prompting me to continue to make purpose from my pain, help others remember their light, and stay on the path of self-expansion and growth, I say YES over and over again. Because I trust that inner compass that has led me all along the way.

There is a power in making a choice to lean into your truth, taking responsibility for your life, and taking one step at a time toward your essential truth. The power lies in choosing yourself, over and over again, despite what the world, society, and others are chanting. When we accept the truth that we are all here on this Earth to do incredible things, the paradigm begins to shift and the world changes. I deeply desire to be part of that change and to see humanity reconnect with the light that lives within.

In my work, I SEE the whole human. I take a fully integrative and holistic approach to work with all aspects of each individual my path crosses. Helping others rediscover that which lights them up from the inside out is one of the greatest joys of my life!

My work in the world is a culmination of my lived experience as well as the avenues to which my heart has been called towards. While working as an Occupational Therapist in the Inpatient Rehabilitation field I was reminded daily of the sacredness of life and a life well lived. Time after time I would be confronted with the realization of my patients', as well as my own, mortality. Knowing that each moment on this planet is a gift and one that should not be taken for granted. I would hear the lessons of life from the mouths of those I cared for and was deeply affected on a heart level by their stories. The high executive who worked day and night to secure a space in society, only to find himself debilitated following a major stroke one week following his retirement. The mother who cared for everyone other than herself, always putting others before herself, recovering from a heart attack following the birth of her third child. The 16-year-old that had been walking down the sidewalk, was struck by a car, and forced to relearn how to walk, live and be due to a spinal cord injury. The lessons of living each moment to its fullest, not taking this life for granted, and realizing that we are worth it all RIGHT NOW reign strongly in my heart to this day.

I have taken these learnings and crafted a way of living and serving in my life that strengthens my heart of service. As an Integrative Lifestyle Coach and Mentor, I help others examine all aspects of their lives. To see what is currently working and what areas need shifting and refining. As humans, we are multidimensional beings. We are worthy of all that life inherently has to offer us, every step of the way. This process first takes the courage to be fully honest with ourselves. Healing the aspects of our lives needed, allowing in a beginner's mindset and heart, and staying open to what is possible moving forward. Taking inventory of the inner workings of lives, assessing what no longer serves, and bringing clarity to what we choose instead. When these aspects begin to align, we can then redefine our beliefs and values to cultivate the version of ourselves that we are desiring to move towards.

This work, the work of stepping bravely into the abyss of our innermost being is one of courageous strength and determination. It's the step necessary to move us forward toward living a life of integrity and endless potential. It is the way back home to ourselves.

I would like to offer an invitation to each of you here, to take the first step down the path of coming home to yourself. To begin to take inventory of how your life is currently evolving. To ask yourself, am I moving in a direction that I deeply desire, or are there aspects of my life that I would like to shift? What is working and what is no longer serving the direction in which I choose to be moving? Take an honest inventory of your current existence. Then be with that for a moment. Allow things to just be as they are.

Then LEAN IN. Lean into your inner compass, asking for guidance and direction… and then listen. Listen to the whispers, the nudges, coming through. Allow the voice of your soul a space to be heard. All the answers live within, they just need a space to land. When you feel yourself looking outward, asking for answers from the external world, pause… reflect… And remember that the truth is not found out there. The truth lies within. Lean in and be patient for the guidance of your heart to make itself clear, because it will. It will show itself to you in the moments that you need it most, stay committed to staying the course home to yourself. And once the message is clear, follow it without inhibition. Take the leap, lean into your truth, and open the possibility to begin living a life of your wildest dreams. You are worth it and it is already yours.

***

To contact Stacie:

Email- stacie@staciebarber.com

Website- www.staciebarber.com

Rod Goodman

Rod is a professional entrepreneur that has taken companies from start up to hundreds of millions in revenue. He's been a Master Distributor, Chief Marketing Officer, and Founder/CEO of many of his own companies.

Pushing limits and swinging for the fence took Rod to the top, but also led him down a path of drug addiction, causing him to eventually lose everything. Early in 2018, he found God and began his own journey to full recovery. He was introduced to Robert "Cord" Beatty and "The Retreat at ZION," in Southern Utah. While there, Rod underwent a spiritual awakening unlike anything he had ever experienced. He decided then that he wanted to spend the rest of his life sharing the ZION message of Health, Healing and Hope with the world!

Rod is now the Franchise Director for ZION Healing Centers, the fastest growing Mental Health Franchise in the Country. He is also on track to publish his new bestselling book "from *Pain 2 Power*!"

Life can be beautiful... Reach *out get help!*

Halfway to Cancun!

By Rod Goodman

My life was such a mess, it seemed like starting over was the only solution... Why not do it in Cancun?

I said to myself, "Nobody wants me here. My family has disowned me." I'd been separated from my wife for years. I was behind on two probations. I thought I was probably facing jail time or worse—maybe prison? I'd lost homes, cars, and countless businesses over the years. It had been a downward spiral, fueled by addiction and self-will run riot, burning bridges and destroying trust with friends and family all the way to the bottom. Why not just pull the plug and run away to a foreign country? Just start over and be free!

"Hell, my passport is still valid, and I speak fluent Spanish," I said to myself—thanks to a two-year church mission trip to Spain at age 19 and a Mexican travel business I started while going to college, specializing in Spring Break trips for students and families. Why not Cancun? I loved that place. It's paradise! White sandy beaches, turquoise water, tropical fish, and beautiful people. I had been there a dozen times with my travel business and recently knew a friend that had made a lot of money selling timeshares there. Heaven knows, I could do that! Maybe I could even find a treatment center there, get sober and work my way into a marketing position.

It seemed like a perfect plan and made complete sense at the time! A whole new lease on life, a do over, a fresh start, all in a tropical paradise! The more I thought about it, the more excited I got! Of course, it sounded good at the time; I was high on crack cocaine. In between hits, I was surfing the net, checking out beautiful places in Cancun. I even found several treatment centers that could help me. I made a list of pros and cons, and it seemed the pros far outweighed the cons.... all in favor? YESSS! That moment, I booked a one-way ticket and a few days later was on my way...

I left without telling a soul—not a single person, not my wife, my kids, my best friend, my business partners, nope nobody! This was going to be a clean break, gone without a trace, vanished. I guess in hindsight, I was fleeing the county. I was running from the law, running from problems, limitations, poor choices, and well on my way to adding "fugitive" to my lofty resume.

I envisioned returning a few years later like a king in shining armor, a new and better man. I had even convinced myself that all my problems would blow over in time and that everyone would be happy to see the "NEW ME." I would somehow come back miraculously redeemed. I was obviously delusional. Later in treatment, I learned this is a common thinking error and addict behavior, it's called acting out of F.E.A.R. = F**k Everything And Run!

Something happened during my layover in Denver. I began to have conflicting thoughts—a real chess game between my heart and soul. Could I really leave behind everyone and everything I'd ever known, loved, and cared about? Panic set in. "What will I do in Cancun if I run out of money or can't get into treatment?" I hadn't really thought things through very well. Addicts tend to NOT think ahead. I didn't even have enough drugs to last me more than another day or two. I started thinking about going through withdrawals in Cancun, possibly living on the street with no place to go. I still had about $2500 in my Bitcoin wallet but wondered how long that would last. Maybe I was making a huge mistake.

What a crazy life mine had become! How did I get here? This wasn't supposed to be my story… Or was it??

I had great parents. I came from a loving home—the first-born of 9 and the son of a prominent doctor. Dad provided all the luxuries in life, including a private plane to go hunting and fishing while living in Alaska. In Utah, we had a 70-foot houseboat on Lake Powell, ski boats, jet skis, snowmobiles, and a 10,000 sq ft winter cabin. During my teenage years, I ski raced, missing lots of school traveling on the Rocky Mountain racing circuit. I won many races, championships, had a closet full of trophies, and served a 2-year Christian mission to Spain at the age of 19. When I returned home, I married my high school sweetheart and had three beautiful children.

I was a gifted entrepreneur. And, at a young age acquired a beautiful home on the hill with two lots, a swimming pool, and several luxury cars. I took trips every month or two to exotic destinations all over the world. I bought my own big boat on the lake with some friends and enjoyed all the luxuries of a charmed life. I was a winner! Life was easy, and I lived by my own set of rules!

Well… they say PRIDE precedes the fall and my life was about to get hard. The quick success went to my head, and I decided that since I had my own rules, it was time to have my cake and eat it too! I started celebrating and living, "the Good Life." I was raised in a religion where we don't drink or party, so to me, the "Good Life" seemed like something foreign, forbidden, and glamorous. For that reason, I only drank when I went out of town. Occasionally at first, but it soon became a regular occurrence and part of the thrill of going out of town!

I attracted a group of friends who also liked to party. We'd go out of town together and eventually to frequenting local bars or clubs. Just a few drinks would loosen me up; I was friendlier, funnier, and uninhibited. I remember calling alcohol the "Elixir of Life;" as it seemed to make everything better. I thrived on being the life of the party and pushing limits. Everything in my life suddenly became physical, the pursuit of material and carnal desires. I got into bodybuilding at that time and started lifting with a guy that owned the Pro Shop at the gym. He got me on all the best supplements—some that weren't legal, but very effective. Then one day, he introduced me to a sleep aid, called "Regenerize." It was to be taken before bedtime to help you achieve a deep "stage 4 sleep" (where your growth hormone was activated).

I remember the first time I took a sip of the salty solution; almost immediately I felt a warm tingly sensation go through my entire body, giving me the most euphoric feeling, I'd ever had. I remember thinking to myself, "I didn't know a body could feel this good." Needless to say, it was extremely addicting and caused all sorts of problems from the moment I started taking it. When it knocks you out, it's hard for anyone to wake you. In fact, this substance became known as "GHB," the "date rape drug" and was soon banned everywhere. My problem was that I wasn't getting a vile of it here or there, I was buying 32 oz jugs of it.

The stuff was unpredictable; at times I would fall asleep in business meetings and someone from home would have to come retrieve me. I once slept for three hours in a tanning booth. The owner banged on the door and was going to call 911 but heard me snoring so he let me sleep. My wife would find me passed out naked on the couch after taking a shower and attempting to get dressed. The concoction would burn off quickly, usually in less than four hours and the withdrawals were terrible, just the opposite of the euphoria. Feelings of nausea, panic, fear, sweats, and anxiety would quickly take over and consume me. At times, I felt like I was going to die. It was so bad my face would even contort and look disfigured. Yet just one sip, and within seconds the warm tingles would permeate my entire body and all order would be restored. I had to carry a vile of it with me everywhere I went, taking a little sip every four hours or so just to be stable. I had developed a real ball and chain. This was my first experience with addiction, and I hated every minute of it. I envied other people living life freely, while I had this deep dark secret that totally controlled everything I did and everywhere I went.

I finally bit the bullet and weaned myself off this beastly juice. However, things would never be the same; it had activated the addictive gene in me, and from that point on I felt the need for something to take the edge off. I drank alcohol, this time not to party but to self-medicate, to manage my stress, fear, and anxiety. It didn't help that I was an entrepreneur, self-employed, with no one to answer to but me no accountability. I was always building a business and swinging for the fence with HUGE expectations. I felt like all my problems would go away with one more home run. I suffered through each day, dreaming of a better tomorrow. I had life backwards; I wanted things to change on the outside so it could feel better on the inside. Later, I learned that our outer world reflects our inner world. For things to change, I had to change on the inside before things could ever get better on the outside. This was going to take some time.

The journey of self-discovery is the greatest adventure you'll ever go on, but it's a process, and experience is the best teacher.

Little did I know, when I took that first sip of GHB and experienced such intense euphoria, that it was going to take me on a 20-year roller coaster ride battling addiction to drugs and alcohol. There would be many sleepless nights, DUIs, jail sentences and extreme loss before I would finally hit bottom, surrender and be set free.

First, it had to strip me of everything: my pride, my business, my finances, my homes, my cars, and my most cherished relationships. My moral character was destroyed. I was separated from my wife off and on for 14 years. She was my high school sweetheart, and at one time, the light of my life. I became a different person once I discovered drugs and alcohol. She would often refer to me as Dr. Jekyll and Mr. Hyde. She would ask, "Where is the good man I married?"

At the age of 60, I found myself homeless, car-less, and pretty much jobless. I was self-employed, working out of the spare bedroom of a friend's house, who let me stay there because we had business together, selling Bitcoin mining to investors. That was until he caught me smoking crack in his house. I was forced to leave his home that day and find a cheap hotel. I was all alone.

Hence… my plan to escape to Cancun!!!

Our life comes down to a few critical decisions we make in a split second that can alter our course and change our destiny forever. This was my time

> *"Destiny is not a matter of chance, it's a matter of choice." Tony Robbins*

I decided to change the meaning of F.E.A.R. to "Face Everything And Rise" and return home. It's not what happens to us in life, but the meaning we attach to it. Change the meaning to one that empowers you.

I wondered if my friend would let me come back. I had nowhere else to go… I called, and he agreed. When I got to his place, I told him everything. How I had betrayed him and everyone that had counted on me. I felt empty, broken, and desperate. I had spent all the money I had been given. He was disappointed to say the least. However, he responded NOT by tearing me down, but by lifting me up and giving me hope! He told me I was so much better than this and how he had always looked up to me. He reminded me of a time years before when he was at his lowest point, ready to give up on life. He had a gun in his mouth and decided to call three people before pulling the trigger. I was the only one that answered that day and what I said to him changed everything. I said, "Do you believe in God?" He said,

"Yes!" I said, "Do you believe God is perfect?" He said, "Yes." I added, "Don't you think God's got a perfect plan for you and your life?" He said, "I guess." I said, "I promise you He does." Now, years later our roles were reversed, and here he was giving me hope and a reason to live.

My friend bore witness to me that God could take this demon from me if I was ready. He said, "If you will just call out to him with all your might, mind and strength, He will take this from you and set you free. He is your Creator. He made you, parted the seas and has the power to do whatever you ask Him in faith. Just do it! Are you done living like this?" I was done. I was ready!

That night, on February 14th, 2018, I cried out to my Creator and completely surrendered to Him. I asked Him to do with me as He saw fit! I was ready to accept His will, no matter what, even if it meant going to jail. I pleaded for Him to take away my craving and compulsion to use drugs. That night, a calm, peaceful spirit came over me unlike anything I have ever experienced. I was given a new heart and woke up that morning sobbing uncontrollably with an overwhelming feeling of love, peace, and hope. God spoke peace to my soul and whispered to me that everything was going to be ok. He let me know that this was ALL part of His perfect plan for my life and that there was a wise PURPOSE to my journey and suffering.

Once we accept God into our lives, miracles begin to happen...

The next miracle God had in store would change my life forever. My friend said we needed to drive to St George, Utah to meet somebody. A week later, he introduced me to a friend of his—Robert "Cord" Beatty who owned, "The Retreat at ZION" a residential rehab center for drugs and alcohol. Cord had his own amazing story, and our lives and personalities were so much alike it was scary! He was a former Hollywood movie producer that lost it all and was now opening treatment centers to help others. He understood me, and I sensed he was going to become an important part of my life. We toured his facility, a 13,000 sq ft Spanish estate bordering the Virgin River. It was an oasis of fountains, ponds, horse pastures, a swimming pool, gym and more, all situated just outside the gates of ZION National Park. For me, it was the garden of Eden, and I had a feeling that somehow this was going to be my new home.

I didn't know how it was going to happen, but a week later, I was on my way to The Retreat. I felt like my life's purpose was beginning to unfold for me. It all started to make perfect sense, why I had gone down this crazy path of drugs and addiction. I began to see how my experience could help others. My mess could become my message, my trial, my greatest triumph. Tears of joy streamed down my face as I realized this was God's plan for me from the very beginning. This was my story!

"The two most important days of your life are the day you are born and the day you find out why." Mark Twain

I spent the next 6 months at the Retreat—first as a student and then as staff, hiking in the breathtaking canyons of ZION National Park every week. It was like walking and talking with God. Feelings that had been stifled and bottled up in me for years began to flow spontaneously. It was like going from living in black and white to vivid color. Tears would well up in my eyes over a butterfly or the smallest thing.

In the end, I wouldn't change a thing. This is my story and I love it! I had to experience it ALL to get where I am. Who would have thought that today I'd be writing a book called *PAIN 2 POWER* and working alongside my best friend and mentor, "Cord" Beatty opening ZION Healing Centers all over the nation. Today ZHC is the fastest growing Mental Health franchise in the country. At ZION Healing, we use the latest technology to restore the brain to proper function along with a course for spiritual awakening— a complete mind, body, spirit, holistic approach to healing that is very effective in healing depression, anxiety, stress, trauma, addiction and more. I'm living proof that no matter how far you've fallen, life can be beautiful again!

At a time when the world needs Mental Health more than ever…

To contact Rod:

For more information about ZION Healing Centers visit www.ZionHealing.com

To learn more about his book *Pain 2 Power* visit www.RodGoodmanLive.com

Isabelle Bart

Isabelle Bart is the founder of Impact Innovator and is passionate about empowering individuals of all backgrounds to create innovative and impactful enterprises. She coaches entrepreneurs to become the best holistic leader they can be in all areas of their life. She speaks on entrepreneurial mindset, abundance, and doing "business for good." As a coach and advisor, she is loyal (no matter what you are going through, she will not let you down), supportive (believes in your ability to succeed), innovative (thinking outside the box is not everyone's habit and will find the right solutions), curious (likes listening more than talking), and courageous (she is on your side and shows you that you can reach what you thought impossible).

Isabelle's experience includes working for the Small Business Administration, providing strategic consulting services to startups, and leading an impact accelerator. In addition, she teaches ideation processes to early-stage founders to help them build successful and scalable companies. She also holds a Master's Degree in Business Administration from ESSEC Business School in Paris.

She has also done extensive work in the nonprofit and NGO sector as the managing director for Academies for Social Entrepreneurship, which promotes the development of social enterprises to address social & environmental problems.

She is a member of the global Catalyst2030 group promoting and working towards achieving the United Nations 2030 Sustainable Development Goals.

Be The Boss of Your Life

By Isabelle Bart

You could make anything you want to happen, even what seems impossible. We all have much more freedom of choice than we think. With a hint of creativity, we can change how we perceive the world and finally get to what we truly desire. I encourage everyone to use the power of inquiry to get to the real bottom of things. What I mean by the "real bottom" is understanding what truly matters to us. We have been conditioned for so many years by people with good intentions (educators, family members, and more) to learn not to dream too big (an astronaut? What are the chances you can become an astronaut?) so that we wouldn't be too disappointed. As children, we had a deep curiosity and kept asking questions until we got a satisfying answer. We should keep asking these questions to go beyond what we think people want us to be and have. In my coaching practice over the years, I never met anyone who desired material things as an end goal. At the absolute bottom of things, we usually seek self-realization, purpose, strong relationships, well-being, and peace of mind. Ask yourself what makes you feel good and which situations and people make you feel at your best, regardless of what society pushes you towards.

We can be proactive and be in the driver versus the passenger seat, where most of us feel content. How do we do this? It requires a shift in mindset, which is easy to achieve if you know how to approach it. It is about framing every experience and every moment of your life, thinking that reality could be different if you wanted it to be.

My story is a story of survival which I had to go through at the young age of 41. Looking back at it, I was very fortunate to be diagnosed with breast cancer in the early stage, and I felt that it was a blessing meant to happen so that I would lead a different life from now on.

Yes, it instilled much fear in me at the time, feeling that I was sick and that my life was under threat, but I also realized that my life was at peril from being resigned about so many things, accepting things when I knew they didn't feel right to me. We force ourselves into situations because we think we don't have a choice. It is not about a choice but many choices and options. It is like any foundation: we will not build the best house if we don't have the proper foundation. The same applies to our choices: in the beginning, if we don't take the time to explore and be creative about our options, we limit ourselves and build a structure that will be more limited than what we can fully realize. The most significant gift that the cancer journey gave me is that in many situations when I am afraid of losing my job or having financial struggles, I always remind myself, "why am I afraid of this?" I survived cancer, and this was much more frightening. It could have ended my life while struggling financially or getting concerned about a new job or project. All these minor concerns would not kill me right away. Instead, this all created a brand-new perspective in life.

How can you build more creativity and change your mindset in everyday life?

Here are some basic principles to keep in mind:

- Failure is good: the more you fail, the more you learn. The quicker you trigger the change, the less effort you are wasting. Success often comes from iteration, learning from what works or doesn't, and making incremental changes.
- Trust your intuition and listen to your body as much as your head. Intuition gets built by all the experiences we have throughout life, so be curious about trying new experiences, new places, and meeting new people.
- Use strategy to set up your goals, priorities, and steps.
- Welcome fun and curiosity
- Take breaks to rejuvenate and do what you like to do to stimulate your creativity. Get out of your place and go to a different town or country if you can.

What does it mean to be entrepreneurial? The word *entrepreneur* comes from the French verb "entreprendre," which means initiate. In French, which happens to be my mother tongue, being "entreprenant" means that you are courageous, and in romance, you are not afraid of rejection but pursue your love targets almost aggressively.

Some key characteristics of being "entreprenant" are resilience, grit, courage, curiosity, and usually a taste for learning something new and exploring. Many entrepreneurs have a spark for adventure. You may not see yourself as Indiana Jones, but I bet you are curious and adventurous in at least one or more of your hobbies (ethnic food, gardening, sports?)

In addition to these traits, developing self-love and vulnerability can go a long way. In my younger years, I attended a very competitive and elitist school, so I felt I had to learn to be the most formidable young woman I could be. How many new moms set the bar so high, thinking they must simultaneously be the perfect wife, mom, career woman, and PTA volunteer?

In one of my marketing director jobs, I oversaw 27 people and directly managed 8. Of course, I wanted to be a role model, know as much as possible about our field and be a fierce leader that nothing or nobody could take down. During my leadership training, I learned about vulnerability and started changing my behavior to show that there were many things I didn't know, that some of my decisions were based on analytical data but still had a part of uncertainty and that I had to learn a lot in terms of effectively managing people. The more I showed vulnerability, the more remarkable things happened to me. I also built much self-confidence, gradually killing my imposter syndrome and fully embracing my strengths and weaknesses. The more I asked people for feedback and advice; the more opportunities showed up at my door.

On the personal side, I also practiced breathing exercises and meditation every morning upon waking up.

Beyond these generic principles, I would like to share more concrete examples of applying that entrepreneurial spirit in the critical facets of life. I believe in incremental transformation through micro steps. There will be times when you feel that you may make five steps forward and three backward, and that is acceptable.

Career/Finance

The career/finance area may be where we naturally think more of entrepreneurship because it relates to our jobs. However, depending on your work environment, it may be effortless to act as an entrepreneur (such as in companies that promote innovation through intrapreneurship), or it may feel like moving mountains, as I have personally experienced in more prominent "corporate-like" organizations that are strict about following processes and procedures. Here are some possible steps to make you live a more entrepreneurial experience at work:

- Ask for projects outside your scope: Companies sometimes encourage cross-functional collaboration through formal rotations. When someone resigns or a position is open, you can temporarily step in to help and learn new skills. Obviously, this is only possible for some technical jobs, but any exposure you may have outside your scope will only bring new ideas and possible ways of approaching problem-solving.

- Do not hard sell but ask many questions, build relationships and understand what people need. The more you listen, the more you build trust with others, leading to more effective and productive relationships.

Social and Romantic Relationships

In social and romantic relationships, there is a fine line between stalking and being "entreprenant." Relationships are not 50/50 in most cases. I have often been frustrated with feeling that I am the master organizer, relentlessly reaching out to friends or dates. Indeed, you cannot sit back and rely on others to take the initiative. You may accept it or simply decide that too much is too much and get rid of some people in your life. It makes a big difference to surround yourself with people who lift you versus taking you down. Here are some ideas on how to be a driver in the relationship space:

- Invite friends to events, and schedule your own, even if they are fundamental and require no preparation like "walk by the beach at 6 pm on Monday, meet at the Pier". Do not get offended if people don't show up, and do not take it personally. Your friends will be very grateful that you are the organizer. Find a way to make it easy that requires minimum preparation.

- Share your emotions, and don't be afraid of the response. I am still working on this one. I want to be as open and transparent as possible, yet I am sometimes scared of bringing up a topic or a question because I am afraid of not hearing what I want. However, it saves you so much time when you stop speculating and ask or say what you feel.
- In love, it is acceptable to say I love you first and shortly after you start a relationship. It is one of the most significant proofs of courage and vulnerability. Many will be afraid of rejection or of appearing too aggressive. If this is the right person, it will likely feel right to them, too, and they will feel relieved that you are saying it first.

Physical Health

With physical health, prevention is vital. We can get so busy that if we experience no symptoms, we are tempted to skip the annual checkups. I can testify from personal experience that it is a terrible idea. I have always been very fit, never smoking or barely drinking alcohol, almost entirely vegetarian, and exercising daily. Nobody saw that cancer would hit me at 41. Thanks to medical technology, I was lucky that breast cancer is easily detected early. I went for my mammogram with a big smile, like a champ who always gets the best results on her health screenings. I fell hard. My treatment was quick and easy. I made sure I knew all the facts, and the medical team did a fantastic job, so I knew there was no reason to be concerned for my life. Here are some steps to consider as a starting point to taking more considerable control over your health:

- Find physical activities you like to exercise and have fun at the same time. Many don't get excited about lifting weights or riding bikes in a dark room. Instead, if you like dancing, sign up for a Zumba class. If you enjoy riding your bike, get a bike and start going on fun trips, or join a hiking group if you prefer walking and socializing (Facebook, Meetup)
- Consider alternative medicine if you have chronic issues to find the actual root cause of your symptoms. I have been a fan of integrative and ayurvedic medicine as I am reading and listening to podcasts on this topic. Holistic health is much more effective, in my opinion.

Mental and Emotional Health

Mental and emotional health is an area many of us don't pay enough attention to. The hardest part of this journey is that you may create a unique, profound transformation, but not everybody in your life may follow. This is what happened in my marriage when, after 20 years of building a family with the same vision, we grew apart when I realized and came to peace with the idea that it is ok for me not to want the same things as everybody else, namely the big house, the comfort, the tedious job with benefits that pays well. I must be in charge of my own life and what I truly desire is not correct or wrong; it just is.

- Write down your vision and goals. You can write it on paper with a pen/pencil as our brains feel different about writing.
- Structure your day to match what feels right to you. For many of us, after going through the pandemic, our jobs can be flexible to some extent. If you work from home, be in tune with your natural body rhythm. For instance, if you are an early riser and feel very productive first thing in the morning, ensure you get your most important tasks done. If you prefer to work out before getting to work, block your calendar to avoid early morning meetings. Most of us also need quick breaks throughout the day to disconnect and let our creativity pick up again. Think about taking a short walk or bike ride around the block and downloading an app to do yoga or meditation. Whatever your favorite, find the right balance, and never feel bad about prioritizing your well-being as much as your job.

Write down on a piece of paper one small step, one small action you will take in the next few days that is different from what you have always done. This could be exploring a new town or restaurant, reconnecting with old friends or meeting a new colleague, or taking a walk on a new trail. Experiencing a small change will start a domino effect in which you will see that things can easily change, get aligned, and flow, leading to outstanding outcomes.

In conclusion, I may not have believed in the power of manifestation until 2022, and yet it has been present with me for the past two years. I went from surviving breast cancer during COVID in 2020 through a divorce and a career change to sharing my thoughts with you here and becoming a writer, coach, and public speaker less than two years later. I am so grateful that I could change my mindset to be in "giving" and "receiving" mode, and I am confident I will keep moving through the universe, making a difference for others every day, and you can realize your deepest desires too!

***

To contact Isabelle:

http://www.impactinnovator.co/ - Book your free appointment and get a 5-step action plan

http://www.isabellebart.com/

http://www.myimpactstrategy.com

Facebook: https://www.facebook.com/isabelle.bart.908

Linkedin: https://www.linkedin.com/in/isabellebart/

Insta: instagram.com/isaquamaid

Kurt A. David

Following life as a professional basketball player, Kurt A. David re-created his successes in education, television, and corporate training, and is the driving force behind Change Like a Champion.

Change Like a Champion (CLAC) is a storytelling, transmedia platform designed to support business and sports professionals in transitioning through life's changes.

In simple terms…change on purpose, for a purpose = a better life.

Leading Change

By Kurt A. David

The Problem - Today's leaders face an ever-changing world. An ability to not only personally navigate the change, but also successfully lead others through the change in imperative.

Why is this Important - The speed of change in the workplace is becoming exponential, and no greater area is this change occurring than in the areas of technology and work culture.

A software engineer once told me that technology doubles its advancement every ninety days. This is partly due to the use of technology, which further increases its complexity and efficiency.

Unfortunately, measuring the advancement of work culture is not quite as scientific, but it is just as important. Culture is a term that defines and governs overall behavior and attitudes, and includes beliefs, values, passions, and often the lens through which we view life, especially work life. With today's workforce environment, developing a positive work culture is important, especially when navigating change, because the adversity that sometimes accompanies change can have a negative impact.

Good News & Solution – Following my life as a professional basketball player, I discovered truths for successfully navigating sudden change. These principles propelled me like a rocket into my next successes in television, education, and corporate training. This discovery during my personal change motivated me to dig deeper into the topic of change, learning there are time-tested principles designed to lead change while simultaneously improving work culture.

By implementing these nine principles, a leader will not only personally possess more tools for navigating change and adversity, but also create a healthier work culture by creating change-ready people that are confident and prepared to change like a champion.

Principle #1

CHANGE HAPPENS – Leaders understand that change happens, and the best leaders are not only on the front edge of the wave of change but also causing it. Before implementing this first principle, one should understand three aspects of the change process.

Why Change – Identifying why the change needs to happen is important because this lays the foundation and motivation for the pending change. During this identification process, the best leaders receive input from all stakeholders that will be involved with the upcoming change to not simply get buy-in but receive valuable input from those who may be implementing it.

What Changes – Clarification and efficient communication about what is changing manages the expectations for those involved. The best way to avoid potential conflict during change is to manage expectations. The best way to manage expectations is by effectively communicating the specifics of the upcoming change.

How to Change – Unfortunately, this aspect can be overlooked because they think people know how to change, however, I've found quite the opposite. Some people lean into change the moment it appears, and others fear it. The goal of this aspect is to provide a process that leads to more confidence for all involved.

So HOW does one change? During my work and research with world-class athletes, I've discovered there is a commonality of success for the individuals that recreated their successes following their athletic championship or induction into their respected Hall of Fame. These five principles not only improved their success after sports but also accelerated it.

Refocusing - Using Your Network - Letting Go - Executing - Having a Mentor provided the 'how' for overcoming the change and adversity that accompanied their transition from pro sports. Through my research and analysis of organizations that faced sudden change and adversity, I discovered in addition to former professional athletes, these five principles helped highly successful organizations that applied them, as well.

These five principles provide the 'how' to change. More details about these principles are in the book titled, The Change – 3.

Principle #2

CHARACTER – To lead through change, a leader has to be trusted. People follow those that they trust, and the best way to develop trust with those you lead is by doing what you say you will do. Your troops will know if you are a person of character and able to be trusted, especially while navigating the change and adversity that will ensue. If you say you are going to be at the meeting by 8 a.m., then be at the meeting by 8 a.m. If you say you are going to do something, then do it. Granted, sometimes a train wreck prevents us from doing what we said we'd do, however, you will lose the trust of your people if that is a recurring theme. That trust is important while leading others through change. Your character matters!

Principle #3

PRIORITIES – Studies show Americans spend 540 minutes per day at work, 468 minutes sleeping, 180 minutes watching television, and 116 minutes browsing the internet or social media. A Google executive once told me, Americans are spending up to 5 hours per day on their mobile devices. It is safe to say, what we do with our time is important. Establishing priorities helps us remain focused on the whirlwind of daily activity, and this truth could not hold truer than when navigating change. A leader must identify and articulately communicate the priorities needed for each step of the change. There is something called a top-down, bottom-up approach to identifying priorities associated with the pending change. In other words, leaders can identify priorities (top-down), but it is also good to get feedback from those who will be implementing and living with those changes (bottom-up). FOOD FOR THOUGHT - there is more information available than ever before in history, yet less thinking. It takes critical thinking to identify priorities and

keeping those priorities in mind while leading others through change will keep everyone focused on what is important now.

Principle #4

GROWTH (PDCA) – This is my favorite part about leading change because it eliminates failure from the process. I used to believe that the opposite of success was failure. Then, I learned that failure is an integral part of success, especially during the change process, and the opposite of success is actually quitting. The best growth model for eliminating failure when navigating change is something called the PDCA process.

Plan – Plan the details (remember Why & What)

Do – Do the change (think How)

Check the Results – Check the results of the process. Is the outcome what you planned or expected?

Adjust – This step is where businesses typically stop and fail, with an excuse of, "We tried it and it didn't work." This is also the step that separates the 'haves' from the 'have nots' and the corporate champions from the corporate losers. There is a big difference between experiencing a failure and being a failure. You are the same leader after your loss as you were before, albeit you can do your best to mitigate any loss or failure by applying these nine principles.

Principle #5

ATTITUDE – When developing a work culture ready for change, we must develop the right attitude. By incorporating the following acronym for the word attitude, a leader can be confident he/she is providing a great role model.

Altitude – Understand that our attitude can determine our altitude

Teachable – It is important to be open to learning through the change proves

Tenacity – Not giving up, fall down seven times, get up eight

Intensity – This is the focus needed to remain on task

Teamwork – Understanding very little, if anything in life is accomplished alone

Unselfish – We're born selfish beings…..think about that sand pale growing up ("It's my sand pail")

Discipline – The best kind of discipline is self-discipline

Enthusiasm – Very little is accomplished in life without passion for what we do

Principle #6

DELAYED GRATIFICATION - We live in a world of instant gratification. If I am unable to acquire something within 30-seconds, something is wrong. Leaders understand nothing great is achieved overnight. We can have overnight wealth and overnight ideas, but truly sustainable change takes time. Shortsighted decisions during change do not normally grow the best fruit, albeit some decisions may need to be immediate to survive a sudden change. However, the best leaders understand there may be delayed gratification when planning more long-term objectives and decisions during change.

Principle #7

SERVANT'S SPIRIT - Our human nature dictates selfishness. Since birth, our focus has been on "MY" sand pail and "MY" stuff. As leaders, we can grow people away from this reality by demonstrating our own ability to do so. The best way to demonstrate unselfishness is by serving those we lead. An added bonus to serving others is that you earn the trust of those you lead, and people do not care how much you know until they know how much you care. Serving others shows you care and can be trusted as a leader, especially during the potential challenges of change.

Principle #8

TALENT SCOUT - Other talent does not intimidate legendary leaders; in fact, they seek and encourage it. During the change process, leaders identify talent that will rocket the team through the pending change. Major League Baseball has created a phenomenal talent identification and development process, and leaders in the workplace can do so, too. The CEO of a multi-billion-dollar company once told me, "We either coach our people up, or coach them out the door." In other words, identifying and developing your talent can strengthen your work culture and resiliency to change.

Principle #9

TEAMWORK - Mentioned earlier, "Teamwork makes the dream work!" That is not a cheesy cliché, but a sound reality and considered by many the #1 reason for the success of organizations. Chatting with an engine engineer enlightened me about the fact that an engine rolls off an assembly line every 18-seconds. Think about that for a moment - and the amount of teamwork it takes to accomplish such a feat with the multitude of changes occurring throughout that building process. Leaders understand leading change is a team sport and utilizing the individual talent of each member can be valuable for the team's success.

As leaders, we face an ever-changing world. Possessing tools that help us personally navigate change while leading others through change is invaluable. These nine, time-tested principles do not simply provide success in the change process, but also create a better work culture by creating change-ready people that more confidently change like a champion.

***

To contact Kurt:

www.KurtDavid.com

www.ChangeLikeAChampion.com

Let's start the conversation by emailing – info@ChangeLikeAChampion.com

Maryann Lombardi

Maryann Lombardi is a business launch coach and author. She has spent the past 25 years working with cities, organizations, and entrepreneurs, building policies, programs, and resources to grow the creative workforce and help entrepreneurs thrive. She now channels that expertise and insight into helping women and non-binary individuals build wealth and independence by turning their expertise or personal experience into profitable businesses.

Maryann is also the author of the book "It's Your Story to Tell: Essays on Identity from a Messy Life Well Lived," published by New Degree Press. The book is about how identities are formed, who has the power to develop them, and why it is essential to be the designer of your identity and the one who tells the story of who you are. She is the single parent of the coolest teenager on the planet. She believes tacos are their own food group, wine is best when it's Spanish and shared, and that it is time for a power shift in business.

The Power of Knowing What you Want

By Maryann Lombardi

"If you don't like the road you're walking, pave another one" - Dolly Parton (Icon)

It is October in Florida. A long time ago. I'm hot and sweaty, buried in the promise of lace and tulle. My 5'9" frame is statuesque, supported by a pair of the most badass shoes to ever grace my feet and the arm of my father. I look spectacular, while simultaneously feeling less than so.

You know the feeling. That disconnect between what your façade presents to the world and what it feels like to truly be you in the moment. Looking every bit the ingenue but feeling like the comic relief. Reaping the societal praise of fitting in the size four but hating yourself for it. Smiling through an inappropriate conversation with a supervisor while all you want to do is smack him.

It is a familiar disconnect for many women. A disconnect almost universally true and equally just as accepted.

I'm standing there at the beginning of a long journey toward something I couldn't quite imagine. I squeeze my father's arm and ask him, "What am I doing?"

He says quietly and calmly, "You're getting married."

I begin to walk.

**

We are born into a world of circumstances and expectations that prescript our identity and opportunity before we can even make a choice about who we are and what we want to be.

There is so much about who we become that we do not choose. For example, we do not choose our genetics, socioeconomic status, place of origin, ethnicity or race, or even our parents' desire to parent a child.

Layered on top of that is a mirage of expectations perpetrated by our parents, extended family, schools, care providers, cultures, media outlets, governments and institutions, and societies.

We stand at the center of that matrix of circumstances and expectations, trying to develop our own personal identity. An identity that encompasses our gender or sexual identity, our goals, or beliefs—the things that we claim as our own.

All these circumstances and expectations weave together into stories that tell us who we are, what we are capable of, and what we can and cannot have. All of this happens before we even think to ask ourselves the questions: Who do I think I am? What do I think I am capable of? What do I think I can or cannot have?

What do I want?

**

I never really imagined marriage when I was younger—never really thought about motherhood either. I'm not sure why. It seems like a rite of passage as a young woman, but for some reason, it wasn't a part of my experience.

I wonder if boys ever think about it—what it would be like to be married or to experience their wedding day. Some of them must. I'd love to see more of those stories instead of the ones that limit the interest in marriage, parenthood, and the rituals that surround them as only a woman's experience.

Although I was surrounded by mothers and married people, marriage and motherhood weren't presented as aspirations. They were givens, maybe even expectations. I didn't feel the pressure for those two accomplishments to define me, but I knew they would or should happen at some point.

**

Too often we move through our lives making career choices (and life choices) without asking ourselves, *do I really want this? Is this part of my plan for me or a plan that was designed by someone else? Am I living up to some expectation that was uploaded to my operating system, or am I making my own choice?*

We get into jobs (or marriages) that feel dissatisfying. Jobs that don't take into account our needs. Bosses who don't understand that addressing those needs would retain their best employees and lead to better business results.

But the corporate work world wasn't initially designed to include women. We end up doing more while earning and investing less. We get lost in the gender gaps that keep us from our financial, professional, and personal potential. We adapt to be more like men, which seems to work for some. But we still struggle to manage the growing responsibilities at work and at home, as the demands on our time and attention seem to populate like rabbits.

It's no wonder we find ourselves screaming "make it stop" into a pillow and dreaming of ditching it all, getting a dog, and moving to Costa Rica.

But the good news is we have more power than we think we do to make it stop.

Webster's dictionary defines power as "the capacity or ability to direct or influence the behavior of others or the course of events." Too often we feel powerless, like the events of our lives and the choices we have are limited. That the train has already left the station, and it is heavy and moving fast and there is nothing to be done about it. It's easy to relinquish our power to our circumstances, expectations, and momentum.

But we are not powerless. On the contrary, we do have the power to influence our own behavior and direct the events in our lives.

We can move to Costa Rica. We can ditch the relationships that don't serve us. We certainly should get a dog, because who doesn't need a little unconditional love in their life? We can also just start by saying out loud: "This isn't working for me!"

**

"It's hard to know what you want when you don't know who you are. It's hard to know what to do when you don't know what you want." - Maryann Lombardi

As a business launch coach, this is the moment people find me. They are done with relinquishing their power, whether intentionally or unintentionally. They want to leave an unsatisfying job and launch their own business. But it isn't really about the business; it is about what launching their own business allows their life to be.

As women, we are sold this lie that we can (and should be able to) balance work and life. All while looking and feeling great and providing our partners and children everything they need—while still bringing freshly baked goods to the PTA meeting. We are told we can have it all. But why should we even want to "have it all?" That sounds exhausting; a recipe for burnout, failed relationships, and probably too much Pinot. What is more important than having it all, is having what you *want*.

My clients are tired of asking permission from a manager to pick up their kids early from school. They are exhausted by planning their life around their work. They are pissed off—always using their talents and creativity to build someone else's dream instead of their own. They want control over their time and attention. They want the triad: more money, more independence, more impact. The businesses they design, the businesses we launch, allow them to do just that.

**

When my child was 3, I remember sitting in the grass, watching their wonder at a blade of grass. We were playing and gabbing about something I can't remember. I sat there listening to them, staring at them. I was fully present with them when two things crossed my mind: I am filled with so much joy right now watching this ridiculously cute kid, and I can't remember the last time I felt this way.

I was so numb and exhausted from the challenges in my marriage that it took all the energy I had to be present with my child—that was no longer sustainable.

That day in the grass, I decided I wanted more of that joy. I decided I *needed* more of it. I started imagining what my life would look like with that joy; what it would feel like. I started dreaming of the kind of life I wanted to lead and knew I had to do something drastic to live it.

And so I did. What followed was a whirlwind of pain, beauty, discovery, risk, adventure, presence, and so much joy. I designed a life around me and my child. I built an entrepreneurial career that made space for my single-parent lifestyle. We moved to a more vibrant place and traveled often. We reimagined our family rituals and rebuilt our community. We laughed a lot, cried too, and developed the kind of relationship looking back I wished I'd had with my mother when I was young. And yes, we got a dog.

My divorce was one of the best things to happen to me. That sounds weird to say, but it is nonetheless true.

**

"I think a lot of people dream. And while they are busy dreaming, the really happy people, the really successful people, the really interesting, powerful, engaged people? Are busy doing." - Shonda Rhimes, *A Year of Yes*

"But how do I start? What do I do first?" asked a woman I was on a call with the other day. She came as a product of overwork who opted out of her full-time job during the pandemic. She was ready for a change and eager to launch a business.

Step One: QUESTION

When was the last time you sat down to ask yourself: *what do I want?*

And I don't mean what do you want for dinner, or what you want for your kids or family. I mean what do YOU want, really want deep down. What do you want your life to look like? Where do you want to wake up in the morning? What do you want it to sound like, feel like, smell like, taste like? Does the country, state, city, town, home you live in sound, feel, smell, taste as you want it to? Did you choose the place you are now? If not, why are you there? If you did choose it, are the circumstances that led you there still the same today?

How about your job or employment? Do you enjoy it? If so, why? If not, what keeps you there? How did you choose the career you are in? Do you find it rewarding? How do you feel when you wake up on Mondays? Are you happy to go to work or do you feel differently?

Write down your answers in a notebook, on your phone—wherever is convenient. Keep a record because you'll want to reflect on what you discover.

By asking yourself these questions, and many more, you'll start training yourself to look at your life with a new lens. The goal isn't to judge your answers, but to observe them. Judgment is the quickest way to slow your progress down. If you spend time judging what you learn or what you write down, you will start "should-ing" all over yourself. If you start labeling what you discover as a success or a failure, it will breed resentment, anger, and fear; that thinking will not get you anywhere useful.

Step Two: GET HELP

Self-exploration can be challenging, especially if you start to discover how dissatisfied you are with where you are, what you are doing, and who you are with. Connecting with a coach or a therapist for a short time can help guide you through these questions or work through any feelings that come up.

I know your besties are amazing, but they are not the only ones to guide you through this discovery. Same goes for anyone in your family. Those people have too much investment in your life as is. I am sure they love you and want what is best for you but it is hard to question and observe your life nonjudgmentally when you are talking about it with the people *in* your life. There will be plenty of time to explore what you discover with them later.

Step Three: TAKE ACTION

Consistent little actions are the unsung heroes of a fulfilling life and successful business. Conversely, inaction is the silent killer of dreams.

The busy-ness of life gets in the way, and before you know it, years have gone by. Busy-ness prevents us from taking a single step to start a business, move to that place we've been dreaming about, write that book, or change our lives.

It's important to remember that inaction is as much a choice as taking action. You can choose inaction, or you can choose to take action now. And here's why you should:

Inaction breeds inaction. The longer you wait, the harder it becomes to take that first step. But once you do take action, momentum starts to build, and it becomes easier to keep going.

Inaction leads to regret. Don't wait until it's too late to start living your dream. Act now and avoid looking back with resentment.

Inaction prevents you from reaching your full potential. By taking action on your business idea or personal life goals, you're opening up a world of possibilities and setting yourself up for success.

**

It can be hard to take the time to get to know yourselves and what you want—but you must. If you don't choose the life you want to live, someone else will choose it for you.

Prescribing our identity, controlling what we should or should not do, who we can and cannot be happens subtlety and not so subtlety. So it is not surprising if you have not been asked what you truly want or if you have not asked yourself.

The idea of actually asking women what they want is a radical idea. Women taking what they want, designing lives and businesses on their own terms, disrupting gender norms and established power structures, building pathways to get what they truly want is all revolutionary.

So why ask?

We ask because we have to. If we don't ask it of ourselves, who will? It is vital that we make sure we are living lives of our own design. Let's be willing participants in the lives we are living. Once we ask ourselves what we want, we will finally know all of the amazing, beautiful, powerful things that are possible.

To contact Maryann:

More information can be found at www.maryannlombardi.com

https://www.linkedin.com/in/maryann-lombardi/

https://www.youtube.com/@maryannlombardicoaching4275

https://www.instagram.com/iammaryannlombardi/

Jason Morris

Jason Morris is the CEO of Listing Alchemy where he helps entrepreneurs transform their businesses through a methodology he calls "Contagious Voice". Jason has a degree in Sociology from the University of Delaware and is a Robbins-Madanes Trained Coach having completed his training under his teachers Tony Robbins and Cloe Madanes. His goal is to use "whole person" coaching to help his clients harness, and bring into alignment, their unique strengths so they can accomplish their life goals without the pain and aggravation created when personal and professional ambitions are in conflict. Jason has sold hundreds of millions of dollars in products and services across multiple industries, has been seen on NBC, USA Today, CBS, and FOX news, and has helped business owners get everywhere from HGTV, to Real-Trends Best in America, to the Inc. 500 list. Jason currently resides in Northern Delaware with his wife Nancy where he enjoys flying, sailing, travel, and hanging out with their two dogs. If you have questions about hiring Jason for coaching or a speaking engagement you can find him online at http://listingalchemy.com, or by emailing info@listingalchemy.com

The Power to Summon
Reclaiming Your Strength Through Directional Harmony

By Jason Morris

I have a serious question for you. When you reach for your power... does it come when you call? For most people the answer isn't so simple. When I ask an audience, I get mixed responses. Sure, some say, "Yes," but the others? Many avoid eye contact and hope they're overlooked. Some fear it. Some despise it. Some give it away, and some have it taken. For much of my life I was in the last group.

I was six. As an Army brat I already knew about moving. Back then, we were a family of six. Mom, Dad, and four kids—plenty to keep Mom busy while Dad was on duty. I think he was Captain at the time but really don't recall. I just knew he had rank, so I enjoyed a small amount of status. As kids, we'd find out whose parents outranked who's, and the pecking order was set. That was just the way it was, and I relished the power. Between that boost to self-importance and a naturally reckless spirit, I got into plenty of trouble.

Now "trouble" was code for "filthy mess." We'd shoot marbles in the dirt or fight sandcastle battles with plastic soldiers. Sometimes we'd sneak into the storage units and pretend we enjoyed filched cigarettes. And of course, there were always trees to climb. I'd come home covered with twigs, cuts and bruises, torn pants, and plastered in muck. Life was an adventure. We made memories and met new friends. But that was also when I met my Demon.

I remember in flashes. Kids shouting and sprinting through the woods. A rickety platform high up a tree. A knotted rope. Kids screaming for me to climb. A cracking branch. A scream. Then the ground whistling up to smash me from the sky. The other kids running to leave me scrabbling at the ground. Dizziness, fear, then blackness. I woke to cool sheets, a squeaking wheel and ceiling tiles passing overhead. Brilliant lights and people in blue gowns. My parents watching from a window overhead. A plastic mask. Hissing air. Then nothing.

A whistle and an acrid stink dragged the world into muddy focus. People spoke as they moved over me in brisk efficiency, but I couldn't understand them. Everything looked wet. The center, sharp and bright. The edges blurred as if looking through tears. I felt my body but couldn't move... not even to blink. There was activity below my waist, and I watched the reflection on a polished lamp as pieces fell together. I was on an operating table. Surgeons bent over my leg where a ruby puddle filled and emptied with the slurp of a siphon tube. I noticed a drill and realized that's what woke me. A hand reached for the drill and panic surged.

It whistled, cheerfully chewing into bone. The stench of burning teeth filled my nostrils as a scarlet Demon burrowed up my leg into my groin then nested in my stomach where it tried relentlessly to claw its way into the world in a shriek of pain. It scrabbled and thrashed, but there was no scream. There was no sound at all really. Just casual chit-chat of the surgeons and the drill whistling away behind the invisible wall while I lay trapped in a nightmare. At some point, a machine started beeping. There was flurry of activity, another hiss of air, and the Demon and I spiraled into darkness.

I woke to smiling faces. My parents sat by a strange contraption with a pulley that hoisted my leg at an angle. A cast ran hip to toe. Below my knee was a clamp attached to a steel rod running through a blood-caked hole in my leg. I jerked my eyes away as images of men in blue, blinding pain and smothering silence flashed in my mind.

It turns out, I fell. I was two stories up when a branch snapped, and I smashed to the ground sending the other kids running. I lay alone until the paramedics showed up, and seeing my leg twisted at a sickening angle, unceremoniously tugged it straight and carted me off to the hospital to drown in a dreamscape flooded with terror. My parents explained that for six weeks, sandbags would hang from the rod running through my shin to hold it still while the bones knit. They said I'd be fine, but I didn't feel it. The Demon squirmed in my chest, and I knew more than just my leg had been broken.

It came to visit me that first night. The ward was quiet, and an orderly's shoes squeaked as he made rounds. I had too much juice at dinner and around midnight my bladder started to nag. Peeing with a full cast attached to a sprung bear-trap was tricky so they gave me a special jug, but I couldn't reach it. I stretched but barely brushed it with my fingers. In mounting discomfort, I started to panic. Suddenly I was back on the operating table. I tried to call for help, but something clutched at my chest, and I couldn't find my voice. I struggled in silence until I couldn't wait anymore. Choking on frustrated tears... I let go. A stain spread across the bright graffiti well-wishers had scrawled across my cast to soak the mattress where I sat all night watching the cheery drawings dissolve into sad little puddles.

They say changing your life just requires you to make a key decision during a significant emotional event. These decisions are subconscious and can last a lifetime. When I fell, the six-year-old me made several key decisions that altered my life forever. Because I was the center of attention when I fell, I decided that attention equals pain. Because everyone ran, I decided that friends would let me down. And because my voice failed and left me helpless in the hands of strangers, some part of me decided my power wouldn't come when I called. I was on my feet in six weeks, but part of me never left that table.

Yet life went on. I don't even think anyone noticed anything was wrong. I only froze when stressed, so it was unpredictable. It happened in class when reading aloud. If kids teased me. When talking to strangers. Once, one of these episodes even landed me on the front page of the paper. It was the first day of school and all the teachers were passing out books; so, by the end of the day, my backpack was stuffed. This was my first time riding the bus, and I waited at the back of a long line as teachers sorted us onto our respective rides. I shrugged my pack to a more comfortable position and a strap broke, scattering school supplies to the wind. The line kept moving as I scrambled to pick everything up. It rounded the corner out of sight. I struggled, wishing for help that I just couldn't seem to call for. I caught the last paper in time to see the final bus pull away leaving me alone in an empty lot. Not knowing what to do I sat down beside the road. Eventually a passing car pulled over and the driver started asking questions. What was I doing? Where were my parents? After getting my story, she got back in her car, and I watched her drive away. The next day I was on the front page of the paper. Apparently, the woman was a reporter. She thought a child left on the side of the road in 98-degree heat was a great story. It never occurred to her to offer help. I never asked.

Over time these incidents piled up. First it was embarrassing moments in class, then with friends, then sports and the locker-room. And forget about talking to girls. Ironically, they found my silence attractive, but the more they chased, the more I clammed up. Life reinforced a belief that I was powerless to act. So, I lived on the outside looking in on a world I desperately wanted to be part of.

The worst part was that on the surface, it appeared I had everything going for me. I had a good family. We never wanted for anything. I got a good education, and when I looked in the mirror, a blond haired, blue eyed young man with reasonably attractive features looked back. Oh... and I was tall. Did I mention that? By the age of fifteen, I stood over six feet. You'd think I'd be happy about that, but it made me the target of plenty of unwanted attention. I never ran or cried. I just... endured. Yet I couldn't get away, so the tension mounted. I developed stress migraines that sent me to the nurse's office. When I came home, I just slept.

My one escape was books. I read constantly. Whether it was fantasy, history, fiction, physics, chemistry, psychology, it didn't matter. I spent hours learning everything from ancient woodcraft to zoology. But I wasn't a good student. I hid in plain sight doing enough to avoid trouble, but not enough to attract attention. That went on until I discovered Karate—rather, Karate discovered me. I was on a learner's permit, and to my dismay, this meant driving my sisters to dance classes. I had strong ideas about being seen in a dance studio, so as intriguing as I found watching the girls flitting about in tights, most days I waited in the car.

One day boredom drove me inside to raid the vending machine. A scream and the sound of splintered wood rattling against a concrete wall brought me to a halt outside a door. Inside were barefoot people of all ages, clad white uniforms tied with colored belts. I watched a student facing a stocky man in his forties firmly gripping a stack of boards in outstretched hands. The young man shouted and drove his fist to explode through the boards and send them flying. I was stunned as the instructor called me over and asked if I wanted to try a class. I found that I did; and suddenly, there I was, punching and kicking for all I was worth.

Then, he called me to face the board so I could "give it a whack." I chopped down, only to have my hand rebound throbbing. He shot the class a look to silence their chuckles. He went on to explain a concept called "directional harmony." He said when I tried to break the board, I was using only one of the five elements of power that, when combined, create tremendous force. Then, he called on nine-year-old Betina, who weighed maybe seventy pounds. She screamed and struck in a blur that sent fragments flying. It was one thing watching older and larger students do it, but when this little girl showed me up, I was astounded. I watched carefully as he demonstrated how to harness and combine each element of power. When I had it, I signaled I was ready. He nodded and said, "Cut the cake." In in a moment that changed my life, I reached for my power and with a primal scream, blasted that board to scrap.

Beyond taking a step toward reclaiming my power that day, I learned something even more valuable. I learned that to succeed at something, you have to learn it's secrets. So, I continued to learn, and practice, and eventually, to teach. Over the years I realized that "Directional Harmony" applied as much to calling your personal power as it does to breaking boards, although there are nine elements vs. five. I believe the full measure of your power demands an alignment of physiology, focus, skills, resources, relationships, purpose, environment, time, and preparedness. And with that level of congruence, you can achieve anything. It has become my life's work to help reconnect people to the elements of their power, in order to create a driving force that transforms their lives. Why go through the trouble to learn? After all, while the spark of re-connection often happens in an instant, calling the full measure of your power is a labor of love that spans a lifetime.

The "why" for me was simply to matter. Feeling that my voice was stifled at a young age, I fantasized about being able to move a crowd with the force of my words. I wanted to feel powerful and to make a difference. The hunger burned in me. Yet for most of my life, it felt out of reach. I was happy any words would come at all, let alone believe that one day I would enjoy speaking to a crowd of hundreds. My "limits" in that area seemed absolute. There was even a point in my journey when I convinced myself that to inspire people, I had to either be rich and famous or have endured some horrible disfigurement to turn into a best seller. From that perspective, I viewed what attributes I did have as working against me. After all, I was tall, blond, blue-eyed, educated, from a good family, and passably attractive. How the heck could I succeed with those credentials? I thought if I somehow managed to survive having my ears ripped off in a tragic lawn-mowing accident, it would at least give me something to work with. Imagine the absurdity. It took me years to realize that with a self-protective reflex to hide from the world, I created an identity around the idea of "I can't." The funny thing about identities is that they feel solid and unalterable right up until the moment you have irrefutable proof of an exception to the rule. When I broke that board, I learned that there were, in fact, times when "I could." That idea was the crack in the dam that allowed power to begin to flow into my life.

I realized I could find exceptions to just about any perceived limitation; so I deliberately set about cultivating a new reflexive response to challenges. Whenever I felt that "I can't" sensation coming on, I immediately asked myself, "What would have to change so I could?" Later, that reflexive question evolved to "what would have to happen to make it easy, and enjoyable? It wasn't until I learned that absolutely any setback, challenge, or circumstance could be turned into a resource if looked at it the right way, that things really took off. I discovered that calling my power wasn't about being talented or outgoing, lucky, strong, attractive, having wealth, or a good family. It was about finding, and aligning, resources so they could be unleashed all at once to achieve a goal. And for the last thirty years, I have been absolutely obsessed with this notion. I realized the early isolation was the resource that instilled a hunger to learn and make me relentlessly pursue the secrets behind just about everything. It drove me into personal development to learn the secrets behind mindset, making friends, and developing influence. It drove me to learn the secrets to sales and marketing and start my first business at the age of nineteen. It drove me to learn how to write and became a published author. It drove me to learn the relationship secrets that won me the love of my life and wife of twenty-three wonderful years. To learn about health, fitness, and rest. To obsess about purpose, fulfillment, and leadership. How to hijack habits and leverage; how to maximize my time and learn the secret to acquiring secrets. But most importantly, it led me to see that my power had always been there; I had simply misplaced it.

When you can honestly claim the mindset that life happens "for" you—not "to" you—everything becomes an advantage. With that mindset, calling your power is never about ability or resources. It's about perspective and resourcefulness. With that mindset, your anguish can become your armor. Your wounds can become your weapons. Your mess can become your message so that battered, bruised, and broken dreams become the breath behind your battle cry.

With this mindset, I have been blessed to travel everywhere from Alaska to Fiji. I've been honored to work with, and touch the lives of, countless extraordinary people from all walks of life. To generate hundreds of millions in sales across a dozen industries. To build teams that have been everywhere from HGTV to the Inc. 500 list to Real Trends Best In America. I've hiked, biked, kayaked, and sailed. I've plunged through ice and stormed through fire. I've learned to fly and soared over some of the most incredible landscapes on Earth. I learned to dive and marveled at the alien wonders just beneath the surface—all to see if I could. I've laughed and cried, loved and lost, and I wouldn't trade a moment.

Do you wonder if my power comes when I call now? You better believe it! And so will yours. If you question that, I invite you to do an experiment. Take a pain you have suffered, or a challenge you are facing, and ask yourself, "If I absolutely had to find some benefit, strength, ability, lesson, opportunity, or relationship that came out of this (or could come out of this if I wanted) what would it be?" If you're stuck, try writing it down. For some of you, the answer will immediately spring to mind. For others, it might take a day or two. Be patient. Maybe you'll be inspired by an unexpected flash of color that triggers a whole new line of thinking or have an epiphany while brushing your teeth. With this mindset, the possibilities are endless. With this mindset, I assure you, when you reach for your power, it will come when you call; because now you know where to look.

Jason Morris is considered by many to be one of the East Coast's foremost Life and Business Strategists.

To contact Jason:

Website: www.ListingAlchemy.com

Email: Info@ListingAlchemy.com

Jennifer Butler

Jennifer Butler is a Jill of All Trades: she bakes, knits, grows children from scratch, builds sheds, and can finish drywall. She is also a budding Author and a Certified Youth Life Coach who has dedicated her life to supporting tweens, teens, young adults, families, and neurodivergent folks to become their best self. For more than 20 years she has been working in the mental health field, supporting teens who were labeled "emotionally disturbed," "troubled," "damaged," and "unwilling." But what she saw was "misunderstood," "frustrated," and "lost" individuals who were never given the benefit of the doubt.

Two decades of mental health work coupled with a decade of schooling and a hidden talent for seeing challenges from a four-dimensional point of view, Jennifer is a fierce advocate and educator around the disparities that disadvantaged communities face on a day-to-day basis. When she isn't fielding questions from her young children, snuggling with her dogs, or watering her house plants you can be sure to find her serving, learning, and speaking out against the lack of justice and inequality in the world. In fact, Jennifer's big audacious goal is to see the end of the School to Prison Pipeline.

In a world where most people say "no" or "that's not the *right* way," Jennifer says "yes!" and "let's find ***your*** way." So, let's do great things. Together.

Broken Wide Open

By Jennifer Butler

Lost in the pages of this book there stands a girl - short in stature, brown hair (sprinkled with some gray), doesn't demand a lot of attention, and might even be overlooked. Inside she is on fire: burning red hot, incinerating the chains that have bound her, ripping off the labels others have placed on her. If you find yourself standing next to her you might feel the heat. She's been told that she's "too much" and she should turn the thermostat down.

I am that girl. Girl on Fire. Too much. Too hot. Unpalatable.

But also . . . Quiet. Shy. Intimidating.

Broken.

These are the labels that have been placed on me - stuck into my skin with pins: pricking me each and every time. Labels placed there by other people looking in and making assumptions based on what they see without asking me what it is that I am experiencing. Somehow, they don't see the bright red droplets of my blood seeping out from under the labels, pushed to the surface by the sharp prick of the pin.

My name is Jennifer. I am a Coach, an Advocate, an Anti-Racist, a Mother, a Woman, a Human, and I am Autistic.

Autistic. The label of all labels. The label that others, looking in, question, poke at, laugh at, and ignore. A label that should be something that I want to run from, distance myself from, shift into a "better" label. Autism is a label with stigma.

Autism is also the label that saved me and transformed me into my most powerful self.

Since before I can remember I have been…different. In fact, my mother thought that she was going to be giving birth to a red-headed little boy when she was surprised by a jet-black-haired, screaming, eight-pound baby girl.

"Put it back in and try again," she said to the doctor.

I suppose it was meant to be a funny, lighthearted story to tell your child as they grew into their whole self. For some reason I just never really heard the humor. I heard "wrong" and "unwanted" when I knew deep down that your mother *should* love you no matter what. Then there was the colic, and the food allergies, and the skin sensitivities, and the general malaise where a happy baby was expected to be.

I was often described as shy to family members around the Thanksgiving table. I heard this label and used it to my advantage when I just couldn't get my clothes to feel right in the morning, or when I felt like screaming at all the noise and the lights. I remembered that I was shy, and I could escape to my room and watch reruns of *I Love Lucy* on the nineteen-inch black-and-white TV with bunny ears on top.

As I grew, I mastered people-watching. I knew how to listen for the shift in tone, body, or gaze. I have the ability to look across a crowded room, make eye contact with someone, and have a full, non-verbal conversation with them. This was especially helpful during my early twenties as I was leaning into my identity as an individual, a friend, a companion, and an employee.

But it wasn't always helpful - sometimes it was "too much."

I routinely made other adults uncomfortable with my ability to read between the lines and call out the inequality, injustice, and hypocrisy that runs rampant within corporations - particularly when you are a woman. A woman who was "shy" and had learned that it was "rude" to make waves because then no one would like you. And I KNEW that being liked was everything - without that who was I? What was I?

Slowly, I learned how to step away from being "liked." Not surprisingly, waves of disruption and discontent followed. Not big ones, just little, gentle, lulling waves at first. And instead of retreating back into being liked, I used all my people skills to guide others *into* those waves, showing them that disrupting the status-quo can be beneficial. It worked.

For a while.

Then I got tired. I got tired of still trying to please people while not being liked by them. I still didn't know who or what I was.

Am I brave? Lonely? Both? Am I powerful? Weak? Both?

The internal self-appraisal walked with me everywhere, at all times. The good, the bad, the ugly: it was there holding me up and pulling me down.

This internal dialogue is what pushed me through the next five years, reminding me that even though I felt like I didn't belong, it was just where I was—and not where I would be if I kept pushing. So, I worked forty-plus hours a week while attending a local Community College. Graduation day was the first time I heard my mother tell me that she was proud of me. Proud that against all the odds stacked against this "shy," "intimidating," "intense" girl, I was able to finish something that I started. I was twenty-nine years old, and a few short months after receiving my AS I would be joining my cohort of transfer students at The University of California, Davis. I had finally made it to the "big leagues."

The next two years of my life were filled with stress, joy, new experiences, challenges, and more learning than I knew was possible. I was dedicated and driven and pointed in the direction of graduate school.

During all that time, from the very beginning of my educational journey, I never once asked for help.

I didn't use my resources: counselors, financial aid office, study groups, professor's office hours, my school's gym, or even my library card! I did not ask for support or assistance any time I hit a wall and felt like the world was crashing in.

I did it myself. I found a way. I pushed through. I was "determined" and "persistent" and "strong-willed."

There are those labels again, and along with them came that trickle of blood and accompanying pain. Those walls I ran into caused some serious damage, and I was too "stubborn" to admit that there was a better way.

I did not get into graduate school.

When I didn't get into graduate school, I gave up on my lifelong dream of earning my Ph.D. in Clinical Psychology. Here was my logic: "I worked incredibly hard to get to this point and it didn't work. I could have asked for more help along the way, but if I can't do it by myself then it is not for me. Anything that I want to accomplish I should be able to do on my own, and on the first attempt.

"I'm just not meant to be Dr. Jenn, Ph.D.

"I'm just me…shy, awkward, too much, not good enough, etc. etc. etc."

I used the setback as an excuse to be small and unassuming. To step back into my "place" and stop dreaming big. Stop making waves. Stop trying to shed the labels. Start believing that everyone else must be right about me. I "failed," therefore I was a failure.

So, at the age of thirty-one I married, took a job that challenged me in ways I never imagined before (both good and bad), and settled into a "regular" life. A life where my dreams consisted of raising chickens, baking bread and making soap. I gave myself the space to move more freely, driven by the urge of the moment and not the dream of a twelve-year-old girl.

Then I became a mother. And nothing prepared me for that. Nothing. I was a mom who couldn't comfort or bond with her baby, whose screams filled me with pain.

I was broken.

This was the phrase I used: "I'm broken." I told people that being a parent had broken me and I didn't know what to do. The first time I stepped into therapy I was infuriated because my therapist told me that they would "hold onto hope" for me while I explained how I felt absolutely hopeless.

I didn't need HOPE; I needed to be fixed. I needed to find the thing that was broken and put it back together so that I could continue along the path of my average, mundane, simple, happy life. You don't offer hope to someone who is drowning. You throw them a goddamn lifeline.

It would take a year and a half for me to find my lifeline. In that time my daughter grew and became "easier" (she still didn't sleep...) and I found the space to breathe with more ease. I also became pregnant again, a decision that was half-made and fully welcomed. I was feeling better, and I could see hope on the horizon.

And then, within weeks of learning of my second pregnancy, I was broken again. It felt just like day-one of motherhood had felt: no joy and no happiness. I was failing as a mother. Again.

And then my doctor threw me a lifeline and put it around my body - telling me that if I couldn't do it alone, she would make sure that it was done. That was her job. Despite my tears and fears I agreed to take the medication that would ultimately lift me out of the pervasive fog that had settled on my life.

One day I woke up and felt myself laugh. *How strange,* I thought. *I haven't felt or heard that for a while!*

I looked out the window of the thirty-foot Fifth wheel trailer that we were living in at the time. The sky was so blue and the sun shone so brightly. I was back. I thought that was the moment when I knew that I was no longer broken. I was whole again, put back together with a drug that offered me salvation from the depths of darkness that had taken over the last eighteen-plus months of my life.

Something happened when I was lifted out of that fog: I began to look around at the wreckage that had become my life.

One beautiful spring day, as I stood outside in the shade, holding my ever-expanding pregnant belly and watching my amazing daughter play in the gentle sun, I took stock and found my life wanting.

I looked up to the sky and said to no one in particular, "How the FUCK did I end up here?" *I was supposed to be a DOCTOR for god's sake! This is not the life I envisioned for myself!"*

That was *my* moment. I stood there and started doing what I do best: organizing, planning, challenging, and clarifying. I *needed* a purpose, a passion, something that would fill me emotionally as well as financially.

I made the decision to step off the path of "regular, normal" life and trail-blaze a new future filled with success, stability, and happiness. And maybe even a house.

This one moment shifted everything. Making the decision to change my future, take charge of my life, and find my truth propelled me down a path filled with hope, passion, discomfort, hard truths, massive learning, and many, many falls. In that moment, a poor, pregnant girl living in rural America became an entrepreneur (something she knew nothing about and had never seen successfully done).

One might think that this is the lesson I am presenting: you can be at your lowest and always start again, choose a new way, learn new and hard things, and come out on the other side winning, thriving, and successful.

Alas, you'll have to stick around until the end to learn the real truth that I am revealing.

It was at that moment, standing outside my trailer, with my daughter blowing bubbles and a babe growing in my womb, that I made the decision to pursue a career as a Youth Life Coach. My long-time passion for working with tweens, teens, and young adults was finally going to be my career - something I thought I had left behind.

It would be two more years before I would see the profits of my labors. I can't describe to you the feeling of having that very first client reach out, ask me to help them, and then put their child in my care. The joy of being able to watch a young child grow, stretch, stand tall, and find a love for themselves. I had made it.

I just wasn't making any money.

Determined not to make the same mistakes I had made in college, I started to ask for help. I hired my own coach. I read the books, I followed the leaders of the field, I signed up for more training. I leaned into all the really uncomfortable things I had avoided in the past. I pushed further and further along a path that I thought was just going to provide me with purpose and money. What I couldn't (or wouldn't) see is that I was sprinting towards me: the real, raw, unapologetic ME.

You see, to do this work - coaching others - you have to do your OWN work. Break down all the lies, mistruths, false beliefs, and unhelpful stories that have been handed to you throughout your life. To help others find THEIR truth, you must first find yours.

Part of this journey is taking a long hard look at each label you have been wearing your whole life and—one by one—make the decision: keep it or burn it.

This is where I found another wall. I saw other people doing this, shedding the ideas and words that were holding them back from being who they were at their truest, most god-like. But I was not having the same success. I felt stunted and broken. I was convinced that I was missing something as I tried and tried to bring calmness to the fire that was burning inside me licking at my insides and making me want to rip my skin off. Literally. Not figuratively.

And the more I pushed to find the thing that was going to help me extinguish the internal blaze, the more it burned and the less space I had to push into uncomfortable places. I felt like I was failing again. Failing to be my best self, failing to do the things I was "supposed" to do to have a successful business, failing as a human.

Welcome to Burnout.

I started doom scrolling a lot and began seeing my patterns in other people. By listening to their stories, reading the research, and taking the assessments I learned that I am Autistic. And the moment I pinned that label on I felt all kinds of feelings: excitement, release, joy, frustration, fear, anger, hope and hopelessness.

Above all else, right then I believed that there wasn't anything wrong with me - I'm just Autistic.

I can't quiet the storm inside my brain and body because I am autistic, and I have been trying to fit myself into a hole that can NOT accommodate the shape and being of who I am.

But who am I?

Enter Burnout number two.

You might be asking yourself, "When is this chick going to tell me about her transformation and how I can do it too?"

This *is* the transformation. This *is* how you do it. There is no magic, happy ending to this story unless you count me finding me (and I definitely count that!). I found *myself* amidst the chaos, noise, pain, labels, and limiting beliefs. You see, my transformation truly started when I thought that I was broken - when I believed that becoming a mother had wrecked me and I needed to be "fixed." Bringing my children into the world didn't break me into a million pieces—it **broke me wide open**. I found new places inside of me that I had been ignoring and/or overlooking for my whole life!

I accepted who I am - not what other people want me to be, but who *I* am. Learning how to walk through the world with this knowledge is hard and exhausting, and it triggers massive burnouts in me.

And that is okay. Without everything that I have experienced, I would have missed out on finding me: a successful business owner, a loving, empathetic mother, a woman finding a way to love without losing herself, and an autistic adult.

It's okay that my path looks different than the majority of other people's paths. Because it's mine. I found me and I allowed and continue to allow myself to grow and push and learn in the way that is best for me.

Here's the short version:

- It's never too late to start again.
- While the path may be hard, there is always a way.
- **You** are perfect. You don't need to fit into the mold to be accepted.
- Knowing yourself is the most powerful gift you can give yourself.
- Ask for help.

Being Autistic was "supposed" to ruin me.

Instead, it lit up the path to finding myself, like runway lights guiding a plane to a safe landing. It is me and I am it.

So who am I?

I am a warrior, a healer, a body of love.

I am love.

I am the ocean: deep, vast, and unpredictable.

I am acceptance.

I am wise and still.

I am more than enough - I am everything.

I am one with the light of creation.

I am light.

I am a goddess on high.

I inspire greatness in others.

I am a stand for those without a voice.

I am unwavering persistence in the battle of equality and justice.

I am categorically misunderstood and what other people think of me is none of my business!

I own everything about me.

I am that forgiveness is always gifted freely and mostly to myself.

I am power.

I am Autistic.

And my mother named me Jennifer Louise.

***

To contact Jennifer:

www.jenniferbutlerlc.com

jennifer@jenniferbutlerlc.com

www.linkedin.com/in/jenniferbutlerlc

www.facebook.com/jenniferbutlerlc

Kelly Bazzani

Kelly Bazzani, BSN, MA Psychology, Certified Master Life Coach & Facilitator is the proud Owner/Founder of Resilience. Kelly hosts her own show and podcast 'Maximum Resilience' on the Transformation Network with Dr. Pat Baccili and is known as a renowned leader in the field of human potential. The Coach Foundation recently named Kelly in the Top 10 Resilience Coaches in 2022. Kelly was also awarded Best Life Coaching in 2021 and 2022 in three counties by Style Magazines Reader's Choice Awards. Kelly speaks dynamically and passionately about her mission and purpose of revolutionizing the stigma around mental health and promoting emotional wellness, all while addressing a worldwide epidemic. Kelly's unique approach encourages clients to navigate life successfully and set healthy foundational principles. As your Ally for Overcoming Addiction, Kelly is an inspirational and motivational speaker, and her educational, powerful, engaging, and inspiring message will change your perception of addiction. Kelly is masterful in teaching how to go from surviving to THRIVING! Kelly is a Mental Health Advocate, and she embodies mental health advocacy by doing and "being" Maximum Resilience as her life work and in her recovery! Kelly's "WHY" is to educate, inspire, mentor, and transform the lives of others with her personal story and life experience of overcoming addiction and addictive behaviors and the steps necessary to sustain Maximum Resilience!

Resilience in Recovery: Phoenix Risen

By Kelly Bazzani, BSN, MA Psychology, Certified Master Empowerment Coach & Facilitator

So, you might ask yourself, "What does that all mean?" To rise like a phoenix from the ashes symbolizes emerging from a catastrophe wiser, stronger, and more powerful! Throughout my life, there have been many catastrophic events that all led to me now sharing my transformational story of Resilience. I have taken all the obstacles I have endured and turned them into my greatest and truest unique gift I get to give to the world. My Cinderella story of overcoming addiction and mastering the ability to soothe my internal pain and free myself from my mental prison is a gift I am blessed and grateful for every day. Presently, I want nothing more than to share this gift with you! I was born to be on this journey, to lead and teach from my wise experience. It is my talent and my birthright. Unfortunately, this was not always my attitude and not always my mindset. I was a victim of my circumstances for a long time with a fixed mindset, always wondering, "Why is this happening to me!?" This thought was because of my intense perfectionism, rigidity, and obsession with labeling myself with specific identities to define who I was.

From a very early age, I knew I was empathic. I felt things very intensely. I also knew that I sought approval and acceptance from everyone around me. I did this by over-achieving and defining success by accomplishments. The problem with this was that while I was so busy seeking validation from outside sources, I completely ignored approving, accepting, and validating myself; this led to the suppression of emotions, anxiety, anorexia nervosa, and alcoholism in high school. These self-sabotaging behaviors heightened my anxiety because I would punish myself if I were not achieving perfection! I went to Arizona State University to receive my Bachelor of Science in Nursing. I became the President of the College Council of Nursing Students and went directly into the Critical Care Unit at Mayo Clinic Hospital, specializing in Neurology at 22 years old.

Many people did not realize that I moved home with my parents during my sophomore year in college because of my alcoholism. I was a master of facades. I had a work façade. I had a home façade. I had a party façade. All these facades while being numb inside and thinking about drinking, drinking, or recovering from drinking. I had the title, though! MAYO CLINIC! NURSE KELLY! I moved back to the Bay Area and was at the highest standard of nursing at 26 years old, stroke and open-heart surgery certified. Then I broke my back, lifting a bariatric patient that had gone into respiratory arrest.

I didn't realize at that moment that my life was about to take off on a whole new trajectory over the next 16 years and counting! After the first two surgeries, I experienced a loss of feeling in my legs and a severe addiction to a plethora of narcotics, benzodiazepine, and muscle relaxant medications. This was paired with crippling major depressive disorder, generalized anxiety disorder, PTSD, losing the "Nurse Kelly" identity that had defined me for years, and my freedom and independence. Little did I know, this was just the beginning of my catastrophes before I would rise from the ashes. I underwent several more experimental spinal surgeries over the next several years, finally resulting in a multi-level lumbar fusion. The medications and the addiction increased. My will to live and thrive decreased. Several rehabilitation centers were encouraged. I attended. I stayed clean for a short time and now realize that I was taking the medication more for emotional than physical pain. I made abysmal choices in my addiction and got behind the wheel of a car more than once while under the influence and abusing prescription medications.

DUI after DUI, and finally, the consequences came. I entered my last rehabilitation center in June of 2014: unemployable, surrendering my nursing license, facing prison, and not a penny to my name. My mother and father had set their boundary not to speak to me any longer. I was circling the drain and still in denial about the severity of my disease. But boy, was I in DIS-EASE! So, where do you start when you have hit rock bottom and want to make a change in your life? I began by getting rigorously honest with myself and telling myself the truth. It was time to stop the lies and stop living unconsciously. Then and only then, I could step into who I truly was, and my true love story with myself began to unfold!

Carl Jung says, "No tree, it is said, can grow to heaven unless its roots reach down to hell." I genuinely believe the dark led me to light again, which is why I can shine it on you today! It was in those moments of darkness that led me on my path to clarity. I sat in that last rehabilitation center and learned emotional resilience: finding our thinking errors. I started to challenge my narrative and belief system. Alcohol and drugs were but a symptom of everything buried underneath my guilt, shame, perfectionism, and all the masks I wore. I got to bring all my unconscious fears and insecurities to the surface and conscious mind and dance with them. My spiritual awakening and life purpose then came to me in maximum security jail because I had cleared out all the old programming and was ready for the new that I got to create based on pioneering my future. I was a year clean when I went to serve my time. My cellmate was in there for first-degree murder, and I was judging her. How was I in there with a murderer when I was only there for DUI's? My Higher Power came to me louder than ever and said, "If you hit a child or family, you would be in here serving the same time as her, so what makes you think you are any better?" Wow! Ego death to heart space and compassion in seconds. It was crystal clear. My complete appreciation for my freedom and the clarity that I would dedicate the rest of my life to being a vessel for mental health and addiction was overpowering! I immediately called my sponsor and had her send me all my recovery materials. We were in our cells for 23 hours a day. For the 1 hour in the yard daily, I was taking those ladies through recovery steps.

I was sexually assaulted in jail on my 35th birthday. I sat there stoic and terrified in the infirmary immediately after because I was afraid to speak to anyone about what happened. I knew in my heart that my message would inspire and motivate others one day as I could relate, empathize, and hold space for their tremendous pain. I didn't know that the trauma would impact and shatter the intimacy and trust within myself and my interpersonal relationships for years to come until I chose to do the inner soul work and healing of myself first. In my worst moments, when I wanted to give up and end it all, I chose to start by not focusing on the whole staircase but instead just the first step. When it all seemed too overwhelming, and as if I were in a bad dream because of my own choices, it was then that I focused on what brought in the rays of light through the extreme darkness:

The James Patterson book I got to read in jail that I enjoyed.

The conversation with my cellmate gave me a new perspective on the freedom I would soon be experiencing.

My new friends made me a sobriety cake from all the snacks they bought together from the commissary.

Those simple yet tangible things gave me the feeling back in my body and mind from the dissociation of the reality I created, which gave me the courage to move forward.

I enrolled and completed my master's degree in Psychology with a dual emphasis in Marriage and Family Therapy & Professional Clinical Counseling. I began to specialize in addiction and interned with my mentor Jon Daily. I was still seeking approval and acknowledgment as maintaining a 4.0 GPA and completing my master's degree were all I was focused on achieving. My mindset at that time was if I at least was successful and followed through on this, perhaps it would minimally erase the mistakes and wreckage of the past eight years. I later learned that you could not hate the experiences that shaped you. Instead of looking at everything through the lens of "poor me," I began to see it as "This is happening *for me*" to make me more tenacious, resilient, accountable, responsible, and humble. My perception shifted, and this was a game-changer. I went from victim to victor, stopped talking about what I wanted to happen, and started on a rigorous, consistent course of action. I woke up every morning and made a conscious choice not to drink or use that day and was grateful I was free to make that choice. Taking action superseded any fear I was experiencing, so I went to a meeting, called my sponsor, wrote a paper for school, and spoke to another person in recovery who was on the same path as me. They say in recovery, there is one thing that needs to change: everything. That is precisely what I did. I changed every place I went to in my addiction. I moved to my school's city to be closer to my education and further away from the memory and temptation of my addiction. I set healthy boundaries around who had access to my energy, time, and resources. I stayed close to my tight-knit support system and began my spiritual journey on deep inner soul work.

I graduated from my Master's Program with a 4.0 in less than two years and was almost three years clean then. I hit many roadblocks as I had completed the 3000 hours needed for MFT licensure but could not sit for my boards because I was on formal probation for five years. I was devastated. At this same time, my mentor Jon Daily had also passed away from inoperable brain cancer, and I had built a considerable caseload of over 40 clients. It was time for another pivot, which is when Resilience was born! I took a series of Self-Mastery classes in the magical town of Healdsburg, California, and became Master Life Coach Certified. So, I opened my own business in December 2018. I named it after my grandmother, Vivian, whose name means "life," and Jon Daily, whose name means "gift." Resilience, "Life's Gift," was born as I genuinely feel we give life to each other. I learn so much from my clients every day. My number one value is integrity, and my clients know that I do not coach or give assignments on anything I have not completed myself or been through in my life. I continued to take personal Self-Mastery classes to learn more about myself and what I learned is that growth and transformation are messy life-long processes. I learned how to respond factually instead of emotionally react. I learned accountability for my past; how I contributed to the problem by reaction or inaction when the problem occurred. Deepak Chopra states beautifully, "Every time you are tempted to react in the same old way, ask if you want to be a prisoner of the past or a pioneer of the future." I knew my answer wholeheartedly! Once I had done that thorough house cleaning of my soul and had my awakening, I was very aware of not agreeing to allow anything back into my soul that felt out of alignment with my integrity, mission, and purpose!

I built Resilience because when I was in the depths of my addiction and living within the confines of hell within my mind of merely surviving, my soul was wise enough to believe that there was a life I wanted to create based in love, light, hope, and everything magic is made of to THRIVE! I wanted to show those struggling with addiction that miracles happen and guide them through their journey in a shorter amount of time than it took me and with much less pain! I wanted to be on podcasts, write a book, speak at events, reach a larger audience, and have a bigger impact! I wanted the ability to reach more people with my story; to use it to remind others that their past does not need to define their present and future moving forward. I wanted to meet everyone where they were and that we all have a choice no matter what the situation. We can go back to safety, which is not the truth, as it leads to more pain and discomfort, or we can move forward toward growth. Every answer lies within us if we observe, notice, listen closely, and trust. I always say, "Wherever you go, there you are," meaning there is no escaping yourself, so the best project you will ever work on is YOU! People thought I was crazy! Kelly, you are barely four years clean? You have $9,000 to your name? Aren't these visions too massive so early in your recovery? To me, being able to reach just one addict and being a vessel to carry this message with compassion, passion, and grace made me feel like the wealthiest woman in the world, and it continues to do so! I posted my story on my website and started sharing my journey on social media.

My shame, guilt, and feeling alone on this path suddenly made me feel like I was making a difference. My vision and purpose were coming to fruition! As Brene Brown states, "You either walk inside your story and OWN it, or you stand outside your story and hustle for your worthiness." Selfishness and self-centeredness is the root of our problem with addiction. How wonderful I get to lead Resilience with selflessness, compassion, empathy, and unconditional positive regard for my clients today in a way that aligns with my values! I know what it feels like to be utterly powerless over my life, and now I know what it feels like to step into my power. In my 42 years on this earth, there has not been one single thing a client has come to me with yet that I have not personally been through. I have been asked, "Do you have any regrets, sadness, or ever feel lonely on your journey?" First, I never feel lonely when I love the person I am alone with because I am my best friend. I have done the work to get here. Second, I can 100% honestly say that I look back on my entire journey with gratitude because every lesson was a blessing. Every trial and tribulation has led me to this exact moment of writing this chapter.

I have been in recovery since 2007.

I have been in sobriety from alcohol for 15 years.

And, as of July 21st, 2022, I am eight years clean from prescription medication.

Many have stood by my side, in the darkest times and the best and brightest of times. As a testimony to myself and them, I coach without bias, judgment, or criticism. Instead, I am guided by my vision, purpose, and values, and it is a privilege and an honor to guide my family of Resilience into alignment with theirs, as well. The most important message I always convey to my clients is, "I will never give up on you."

Vision

To promote emotional wellness, embody healing, and remove the stigma from mental health and addiction.

Purpose

To manifest healing and positive change for my clients and me so that we see the possibilities available to us in a way that is aligned with integrity, embodiment, and mindful service.

So, who am I, you ask?

I am a beautiful story of hardships, traumas, catastrophes, failures, scars, brokenness, and loss, all woven into deep inner spiritual soul work and healing. The result is a life-long process of growth and transformation leading to the best version of myself so that I can live an empowering life of freedom, resilience, grace, and humility. I will continue to pick up the lamp within to light the way for love, light, hope, and everything magic is made of! My soul will continue to SHINE from the inside out, leading the way for others so that they too may discover their light and SHINE ON!

***

To contact Kelly:

Kelly Bazzani Bsn, Ma Psychology, Certified Master Empowerment Coach:

kelly@myresiliencecoach.com

916-877-8249

Resilience Website:

http://www.myresiliencecoach.com

Transformation Network Site with Kelly's YouTube and Podcast links:

https://www.transformationtalkradio.com/show-details/maximum-resilience-with-kelly-bazzani,387.html

Kelly's Media Site:

https://www.myresiliencecoach.com/media

Instagram:

www.instagram.com/kellybazzani

Facebook:

https://www.facebook.com/kelly.bazzani

Business Facebook:

https://www.facebook.com/myresiliencecoachCA

LinkedIn:

https://www.linkedin.com/in/kelly-bazzani-7181391b4

NEW WEBSITE COMING SOON!

https://www.kellybazzani.com

Lisa Renee Jones

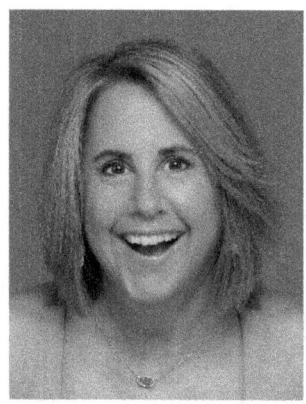

Lisa Jones is a successful high-performance coach with a business and wellness background.

She is president of LR Coaching, a holistic life, and leadership coaching practice. She has been a presenter for the American Business Women's Association, The Health Coach Institute, Voyage Jacksonville, Stand Tall Life Coaching and has also been interviewed on EWTN radio.

As an entrepreneur, wife, and mother of three, she has vast experience and demonstrated a history of working in the business, wellness, and fitness arena. She spent 13 years with Cellular One of Washington Baltimore and Southwestern Bell in Dallas, TX, before starting her own business. In addition, she has guided others in her holistic coaching practice for the past 20 years, helping others achieve maximum potential.

Lisa believes putting in more hours is not the answer to your growth goals. Instead, your path to exponential success means infusing your hours with more quality. Lisa sees the body, mind, and spirit as interconnected systems working harmoniously. When Lisa is not life coaching, you'll find her participating in her other passions: cooking in the kitchen with her family, hiking out on a trail, walking on the beach, or volunteering at church.

Lisa will help you clarify your vision, bust through self-doubt, and create the next step in your journey. Her desire is for you to live the life you want rather than the one you only dream about living.

Stay At Home Mom to Six Figures

By Lisa Renee Jones

I have learned two essential things over my long career. First, you may think where you are right now is where you'll always stay, and second, what a great sense of humor the good Lord has! In 2001 I became pregnant with my first child. I had been in corporate America for 13 years working for Southwestern Bell Mobile Systems, and I told my husband, "I want to stay home and raise our child." He freaked out as 40% of the household income would go away, but we trusted what was to come, and I became a stay-at-home mom. After about a year, I had somewhat of an epiphany. I was practicing yoga at home and realized what an incredible benefit this had been to me over the years, especially during my pregnancy. Coming from a corporate training background, I said, "I need to share this with others!" Thus began my foray into holistic, healthy living.

I studied with some of the top names in the business, began looking into organics and supplementation before it was the "buzzword" of the day and within a year, started my first part-time business. I was teaching yoga locally at a few locations and, after seven years in, advanced this portion of my career by getting involved with the International Association of Yoga Therapists. I was absolutely fascinated by the fact that physical therapists, doctors, and nurses were all practicing yoga and doing their best to bring this mind/body work to "western medicine." I began understanding the therapeutic benefits of assisting others outside the classroom and launched a new wing to the current classroom model. I had clients referred to me by doctors, and I taught pre-natal yoga at the local hospital. Fast forward another seven years, and in 2016 I had remained primarily a stay-at-home mom. I was a yoga instructor and yoga therapist in the area for 15 years, working at various studios and renting a space of my own, always keeping my family first. I worked maybe 3-5 hours a week and only charged 10.00-12.00 per class or $50.00 for private sessions.

At this point, I had my self-study of clean eating and supplementation for years, and I noticed that many of my friends and family were calling me for "health" related issues and guidance. Also, during this time, my husband lost his job for the second time in two years. At this time, he had been in information technology, which was very shaky as quite a few positions were being outsourced overseas. Since I had previously worked in corporate, he asked if I would consider returning to work full-time within a corporation again.

Having three daughters at home, two in middle school and one in high school, they still needed to be our priority. A friend suggested I research health coaching saying it would be a perfect fit. I discovered an accredited institute and completed a 6-month health coaching certification followed by a one-year master life coach certification. Going through this accreditation process was a HUGE affirmation of all the studies I had done on my own over the years. My husband would tell you the excitement he saw in me when I explained what I discovered in my studies.

I was required to take two people through the entire curriculum for my certification. These were known as "practice clients." The decision was left up to us if we wanted to charge a fee for these two clients. Because I knew I had been coaching for many years, I boldly asked for payment from the two practice clients required to receive the certification. I had no issues receiving these fees; they were way higher than anything I ever brought in from my years as a yoga instructor. Life coach mastery helped me continue to evolve and reach full solopreneur status. Mastery gave me the tools to shift into realizing I was already life coaching along with health coaching for years. Mastery allows you to dig deeper into your coaching practice and assist clients in all facets of their life.

As a master life coach, I combine my years in corporate America with my holistic practice and eleven years in marriage ministry to meet my client's needs. There are three main "doorways," as I like to call them, my clients walk through to begin life coaching. They are your career or business, health issues, and relationships. As a coach, I consider myself a human potential specialist, and it's my job to assist my clients in achieving their highest potential.

One of the best quotes I like to reflect on is, "Crisis is not the enemy. It's an invitation." That was my story. My husband and I were in crisis mode. We had three young children at home, and I had left corporate years ago, and I knew I did NOT want to be gone every day from eight to five. My husband was the primary breadwinner; we now had income fluctuation for two years. He was anxious, and our debt was rising. As a spouse, I listened to and heard where my husband was with our situation. Finally, at age 51, I took a bold step to evaluate what I really wanted to do.

Going back to school and launching a full-time coaching practice allowed us to pull up and out and no longer have to say "no" to our children for sports or activities or travel because I could support my husband and the household income. I also set an incredible example of perseverance for my daughters in times of trial.

Six years later, I can say, "I create the life I want to live." Whether I work five hours a week or 30 hours a week, entrepreneurship allows us to plan for future weddings and worldwide travel, and now we live one mile from the beach.

Alright, so let's dig a little deeper into the story – has it been an easy path overall? No, not at all. There were many challenges I had to overcome. Owning your own business means you are on a constant roller coaster of peaks and valleys. One of the main struggles along the way was honing in on a brand. As a solopreneur, it is what makes you, you. There is no marketing team to assist you. You are the marketing, finance, quality assurance, implementation, and delivery departments; sometimes, that can be highly challenging. Life is full of transitions and transformation, and I've had my share. At its core, LR Coaching is for women and men who don't want to play small or play from someone else's script.

Stress management and self-care are of vital importance today. As a type-A driver-driver, I am so grateful that I was introduced to the world of holistic health in my twenties! Thirty years later, I've spent years with some of the best leaders in the mind/body world of health and healing, as well as leadership and business. I have over 500 hours of training and certification in yoga, prenatal yoga, meditation, spirituality, coaching, leadership, and employee work-life balance.

After I returned to the "job force" from my stay-at-home mom years, I realized that adults had lost the ability to relax and have fun. We are master multi-taskers and are on the go constantly. Therefore, we need to learn how to "be" so that we can be all we are meant to be for everyone and everything else that is so important to us.

As a life coach, there is one thing that I LOVE, and that's the TRANSFORMATION I see in my clients when they have their AHA moments and rise to who they were fully meant to be. Some of us are simply infused with the confidence gene, and it comes quite easy. However, others will need to peel back the layers to discover all they have accomplished and no longer hide behind a façade of "I'm not X" and fully step into the "No, I AM "X"! and I do have a LOT to offer this world!"

It reminds me of Jane (not her real name). She was in IT for years, lost her husband, was left to raise her daughter on her own, did corporate work, remarried, scaled back to part-time work to be with her daughter, and then her daughter went off to college, and now she was lost. She forgot who she was and what she had to offer the world. Her skills amazed me; she just forgot how to use them.

Together we created exactly what she wanted. She became a college process coach and now helps other families prepare to launch their children! Her rise was robust! At many points in life, a "thought" alone is incredibly powerful. Each day, over 100 times, we choose to either be positive or negative in our thought process. However, we do have the capability to work through the negativity with an influx of energy to discover "where is this coming from and why?"

Working as a manager for Cellular One in Washington/Baltimore and at Southwestern Bell Mobile Systems in Dallas, TX, I've had teams of up to 20 and trained up to 800 employees. Each person has a unique but identifiable behavior, comfort zone, and social style. We as leaders need to recognize this and work within these "zones." Using these years of experience, I have brought all this to the table in my coaching practice. Guiding and leading people is a gift and requires wisdom, knowledge, and being open to challenges.

As leaders and managers, we need to recognize how to identify and classify each of our employees/clients so that we can have a reasonably accurate picture of who we are relating to and mentoring. Once we are aware of these unique styles, we can move into needs and expectations and strategize what works best for that particular employee or client. After all, we both want to wind up in a win-win situation.

The Building Blocks of Success

Success is strategic. Two components contribute to your strategic success: your values and behavior. Identifying and measuring values is like goal setting in that much has been written on the subject. To create strategic success, you need an understanding of your values. Your values shape what you do. They are established by what you believe is right, wrong, true, false, acceptable, unacceptable, appropriate, and inappropriate. As you have lived, you have developed deep, strong opinions, and your opinions spring forth your values.

The list of every value we have can be very long to the extent that you may need help dealing with all of them. Values shape what you do; after all, what you do creates your strategic success. So, if for that reason only, being aware of your values and being able to state them is essential. As you can tell from my story, I value keeping my family a priority. Some of the things you do will be more important than others. However, it is the values you have that dominate the things you do that are relevant to the creation of your success. This then leads to the second building block of strategic success.

This second building block is your behavior. A coach's primary responsibility is to ensure you are getting into action. In other words, the things you do. These things you do, or your behavior, have a significant influence on creating your strategic success. There are five categories of action I want to share with you:

1. **Work Ethic**
2. **Integrity**
3. **Your Judgement**
4. **Courage**
5. **Willingness to Serve**

Looking at each of these in more detail we will start with **work ethic**. Regardless of where you work (at home, in an office, at a restaurant, Uber, etc.), you will still occasionally seek the assistance and support of others and specifically want them to be willing to exceed expectations. Your work ethic needs to demonstrate that you are willing to do what you ask others to do. The most visible elements of your work ethic are the things you do that impact the time and effort of others around you. These may be relatively simple, like being on time and keeping appointments. Being late for meetings or deadlines creates a poor definition of your work ethic. Some things to ask yourself: Do I proactively move forward on what needs to be done? Do I wait to be told what to do? Be someone who initiates action. They are considered more participatory and opportunity oriented.

Integrity is about keeping your word, communicating honestly, and doing what you say you will do, even when it's hard. People of integrity make decisions about doing the right thing. Doing the right thing when there is little at stake is easy. The real test comes in times of temptation, stress, and pressure. You will be closely observed during these times, and your actions will become part of your strategic success. If you make a mistake, admit it. Your word is your bond, and that is core to integrity.

As a leader or employee, your **judgment** is directly linked to the welfare, safety, and general well-being of others. If you fail to consider the needs of others, it creates a negative perception and sends the message that you don't care about others. Individuals will resist trusting and giving emotional support to anyone who demonstrates poor judgment in their daily decision-making. On the other hand, when you establish good judgment, you are considered levelheaded and authentic. Someone with good judgment handles pressure with grace and, most importantly, with confidence. Demonstrate this, and you will inspire others to handle pressure similarly.

The best example of **courage** is how you handle adversity. As I tell my clients, there will always be "something." How we address that "something" makes all the difference. That "something" could be financial, marital, or health issues, to name a few. No one is invincible, and mindset is key to demonstrating courage. My clients who come to me as they battle a cancer diagnosis are perfect examples of courage. As I walk the journey with them, I remind them that the diagnosis does not define them. What defines them is their purpose, and that purpose does not change. In the scientific community, it is well-known that those who remain focused and involved during their treatment have a higher rate of success in their outcome. So be you, even in the face of adversity.

Most outstanding among the building blocks of success is your **willingness to serve.** If you want others to help you, you must be willing to help others. Supporting and appreciating others in this sense goes beyond just thanking someone and sending out birthday cards. Serving others means that you know what they want in life, both personally and professionally. It means not only supporting individuals but also means supporting causes you are passionate about. It means investing your time and your treasure for the greater good of another, your community, country, and the world. Sometimes it may be as simple as the proper conversation during a difficult time. Helping others does not have to involve considerable effort or expense, and you certainly can't be the solution to everyone's problems or take responsibility for their hope. However, your willingness to invest in another person's life or a cause near and dear to your heart will become a significant building block in your strategic success. Come from the heart. Your "inner knowing" will never disappoint.

Transferring the Building Blocks of Strategic Success

Conveying these building blocks engages the way you communicate with others, and communication transcends mere words. Many people treat communication as a collection of skills. Communication has great significance in facilitating execution. Remember, your values and behavior are the building blocks of strategic success. Strategic communication involves the actual transmission of those building blocks. Whether working with individuals or on a team, your communication must impact others' beliefs in themselves or the project at hand. As a leader, if that applies to you, you must communicate vision, strength, and opportunity.

You must communicate value.

Results and growth. The win-win I spoke of earlier. What's one thing that you could be doing for yourself that you're not? What is one thing that could increase your sales, energy, or connection to the most critical person in your life? Most of us know what to do – we just don't do it. And that is where I come in. To assist in getting you into action. No more excuses. You can't understand what you want without clarity and focus. Just begin. Take an honest look at where you are right now, then compare it to where you REALLY want to be. Can you see it? Let's go!

***

To contact Lisa:

Website: www.lisarjones.com

Email: Lisa@lisarjones.com

LinkedIn: Lisa Renee Jones|LinkedIn

Molly Milinkovich

My work is the result of looking back: looking back at an extremely varied background and acknowledging how each experience—each moment—molded a reality, and a future. I have been on a path of self-discovery since my early years, and I love to share it.

My mission is to create moments of discovery and clarity for others in their personal lives and as leaders in the world. Because when I discovered that it doesn't have to be *hard*, life began to work and the impact I can make became clear. I want nothing more than to share that with the world.

I believe that connection is the pivotal element that allows us to thrive in any area of life: connection to others, to ourselves, to the earth. It fuels me as a mother, friend, planetary contributor, and professional.

Moments

By Molly Milinkovich

My journey of self-inquiry and discovery has been, at the very least, robust. Some of my experiences have been synchronistic, and others are very planned and calculated. I am a life-long learner and value every opportunity I've had to learn more about the world and my space within.

I was raised in a Lutheran household with ever-present formative practices as a child. We attended church every Sunday, prayed before meals, and had an extremely close extended family. Both of my parents were teachers, and a love for learning was instilled in me at a young age. Books were considered a reward in my mind, and I looked forward to trips to the bookstore with my mother. Although I grew up in a small town in southern Minnesota, my mother made sure my brother and I experienced theater, art, and the world beyond our tiny town. It is no accident I've lived a life filled with self-inquiry and life-long learning.

I began my ever-winding career and educational path at Gustavus Adolphus College. Honestly, I studied psychology as an undergrad because I wasn't sure what I wanted to do, and understanding human behavior felt like a great place to start. At the culmination of my degree, I got a job working in a psychiatric facility for youth. One evening, I found myself holding a six-year-old boy who had burned down his house. He was crying for his mother and needed soothing; he was afraid. I was disciplined for breaking protocol and, at that moment, decided that my instincts would be an issue in this line of work, and I left that job.

Purely by accident, I ended up as a children's minister at a massive Lutheran congregation, curating programming for 3,000 youth and training 100+ volunteer teachers. During this time, I attended Seminary. I was raised Lutheran and had never questioned my faith until this point. I began to study the Bible in a way I had never done before, with an academic mind. After studying the historical aspects of Jesus's life in Israel, I decided that my relationship with Jesus was purely intellectual and historical. I left Seminary and decided to pursue my MA in Education. My spirituality was entirely up in the air; it was the first time I had thought about what it all meant.

After Graduate studies, I began teaching 4th grade. During this time, I found yoga. My relationship with yoga started as a purely physical pursuit which evolved into a love of the practice. I was interacting with the world around me differently; I was exploring mindfulness and how I could bring these insights into the classroom. I became certified in the MindUp curriculum with the Hawn Foundation and began teaching yoga and meditation to young people. During this evolution, I became frustrated with what was being taught in public schools. I wanted to discuss the human experience with these children; it became apparent that a mainstream classroom would not be for me.

Around the time my frustrations peaked, I was immersed in the yoga community. A new brand, lululemon, was making its way into the area, and I was very intrigued. So when they asked me to join their team, I left the world of education to join a remarkably different world, not knowing it would completely change my life.

About three weeks into my role as a manager at the lululemon store at the Mall of America, I discovered the internal leadership development team and programming. I immediately reached out to the director of possibilities and asked to be a part of what she was creating. That email led to the discovery of a mentor in the world of leadership, energy work, and self-inquiry. I poured myself into learning personal responsibility and how my energy impacted those around me. I spent weekends in intensives learning about Geotran and how to care for my morphogenetic field. I continued my study of different religions and spiritual practices. Eventually, I created my leadership coaching business based on the premise that you cannot lead others, much less an organization if you are not leading yourself effectively. I found clients who understood the value of spirituality and energy in their businesses and personal lives and tapped into a new way of working within the world. I continue to work with clients in this manner today.

For years I had been asked to study yoga and become a teacher. My answer was always the same, "I am happy with my practice as it is," until last year. As I sat outside the yoga studio, one of my most respected yoga teachers asked what was next for me. I replied, "I honestly don't know." She, of course, suggested I join the next round of yoga teacher training, and this time the word "yes" came to me as my response. I spent five weeks in a 300-hour intensive study of yoga, its origins, its philosophy, and its activism with men and women from across the globe. As the time ended, it occurred to me that this was my path forward. I was understanding the human experience from a more spiritual lens to bring a holistic approach to mental health.

To bring light to how this lands in my personal life, allow me to backtrack to 2007 when I became a mother to the most outstanding teacher I have ever had. I fully understand how cliché that sounds, yet it is the absolute truth. My son came into this world with an open aura, allowing some dark energy to cling to him. At a very young age, he asked questions and shared things he saw and felt, and I knew I needed to understand energy fields and protection on an entirely different level. He intuitively gravitated toward crystals and their strategic placement around his room and our home; he asked for protection while he slept. So I sought out energy healers and learned to clear physical spaces and protect them. As he has grown into a teenager, he has big emotions and is very candid about processing them. I am blessed that he comes to me with questions and inquiries about his depth.

As we have navigated the world and public school system, it is clear that there has been a way of caring for individuals based on outdated information and a very narrow pathway. This operating method has not worked for us, and I am confident we are not alone in this experience. It brings my relationship with family, education, spirituality, and the world, full circle and creates a path of purpose.

I believe the work of East-West Psychology is pivotal to this new generation of expansive souls navigating the world in an entirely different way. I have begun to explore children's access to information and the world's access to them in new ways. I would like to know the impact of this global way of living. How can it be a beautiful tool for understanding? How do we work within mental health and healing in a more expansive way to provide new understanding to an entirely new generation?

These questions landed me in a Ph.D. program in East-West Psychology, exploring what can be created through a new way of working in the mental health world. I continue to dive deeply into ancient teachings and how they impact how we interact with the world as fully expressed humans.

Goal setting has always been at the center of my coaching practice. It was one of the first things I would focus on when working with individuals. However, with limited front-end work, I often landed in the middle of a set of goals with someone who needed more context.

Years ago, I was working with a client on their individual goals and strategies to achieve them in their desired timeline. Their goals included things such as running a marathon and getting promoted, which were not horrible goals by any means. However, as I began to coach them on their minor deliverables, I could hear that the daily steps required to get to the desired outcome were things that would completely drain them. While I know there are elements to working hard that don't always seem "fun," how we spend our days getting to those goals *does* matter! As I listened to myself coach this individual, I could hear my thoughts about *my* goals feel the same way. How many of us were living our lives for someday? What was missing from this practice and the culture of goal setting in which I was so immersed?

I took time to think about how I wanted to approach this conversation with my clients, and, as I usually do, I began to try things out on myself. I remembered a list I had seen somewhere of core values. I dug out the list and began to sort them out based on how excited they made me. Did I read the word and have a million ideas pop into my head, or did I read the word and feel nothing? I continued to evolve this process until I had created a system to replicate the experience for clients to identify their core values. We spend time exploring what kinds of behaviors are reflected daily for them personally to know their values are alive and well. Then it is time to look at goals and minor deliverables and see what, if any, overlap. If goals do not overlap with core values, are they the goals they have chosen? Or are they things they think they should be doing? This practice has become a critical starting point for individuals and organizations, no matter how we work together.

Knowing what is important to clients is the only way I know how to move forward in a direction that will get results.

True to form, this practice has been seamless until recently when I found myself wondering why I didn't have anything I would classify as a "check off my list" kind of goal this year. My days have been full, and I am working toward things that matter to me, where were my gold stars? Again, I began to evolve the practice, realizing I needed to incorporate a new way to acknowledge myself and my clients for my work. Enter the addition of gratitude to the core values program. Taking time to reflect on what's working is the icing on the cake, especially when creating a life that works and is fulfilling.

During a recent core value coaching session with a client, he was coming up with nothing. Nothing was inspiring him; he was extremely down on himself and confident that everything he attempted would fail. This is a full stop for me as a coach. Rule number one is no creation from a place of fear or distrust. There are a plethora of ways I typically approach this type of block with individuals, and it was clear to me that this was going to be heavier lifting than my usual go-to solutions. One of my favorite things is running into situations with clients where what I have been doing requires some tweaking. I love creating solutions and programming that emerge for an individual because it usually means the world needs it.

What emerged from this process was a new program giving individuals and organizations the ability to get out of loops of destructive and negative thought patterns. Who doesn't need that in the world right now? I know I do. He had experienced this before with books, podcasts, and other individuals telling him to simply "change his thinking." He knew this had become such a deep pattern for him; it would take more than a change of heart to undo this learning. He needed tangible strategies and reliable systems in place to catch him in these patterns and adjust. Knowing my relationship with depth spirals, I decided to dig deeper into this part of the process. I am passionate about how we relate to our personal experiences of dark times and interact with the depths of our psyches. I encourage not only creating new neural pathways for an elevated living but healing the parts of us that no longer serve us as well. I encourage individuals to look at their lives holistically and incorporate tangible ways of doing both aforementioned elements.

What would happen if we looked at them instead of asking him to override his relationship with these dark and disruptive thoughts? How would it feel to sit with them for a minute and acknowledge how they have been serving him? In this process, we were able to uncover that this place of darkness was keeping him safe from actual failure in his mind. By assuming he had reached his peak and that no one should expect anything greater from him, he could keep his life as it was with no risk involved. In this discovery, he realized that this way of living was exactly why he had sought out coaching in the first place. He didn't want to stay where he was. He wanted to do more, but he was simply afraid. Most of us, myself included, can relate to this on some level. However, if we take the time to think about it, there is an area of life in which we hold back based on fear. After several weeks of working through his negativity loop, we finally revisited the core value work.

That session was the most dynamic work I have seen out of a client in years. He was inspired and excited about taking risks and believing in himself again. It was inspiring to remember that we all have the capacity within ourselves to create this spectrum of growth. What I know about the human experience is that he will likely experience doubt again. Perhaps he won't see the progress he is hoping for after his first few weeks, and his negative thought patterns will creep in again. What is beautiful about having taken time with these thoughts is that he has decreased the amount of time he will need to spend with them the next time this happens. Every dip will have a shorter recovery time; I know this because I have experienced it. The more familiar I am with my least fun thoughts, the less scary they are to me. This ability to get familiar with our entire spectrum as humans spans the range of individual development to team development and organizations. When you identify and demystify unhelpful loops within a structure, whether large or small, it allows for them to be moved through to a place where productivity and excitement can exist again.

My work as a coach and student of progressive mental health continues to evolve as we learn more and more about the human experience. My work in East-West Psychology allows me to examine the path of human growth in a new way. Every individual's experience of life is, at the same time, unique and authentic. One life cannot be measured compared to another, yet we can all learn from each other on our journeys. As I work with individuals and organizations, I know this work will continue to reveal itself. And for that, I am excited and grateful. While we know a great deal about the human experience, there is still a magical world within each of us waiting to be discovered. This is the work I am passionate about and value.

I am a mother, coach, learner, and passionate advocate for creating an exceptional future for the generations following us. I've got a vision that this future is a time when our educational system is created to educate the body, mind, and spirit of our planet, leaving us space to learn and develop throughout our lifetimes.

If you desire to explore a new way of relating to your personal human experience or feel the traditional methods of looking at personal development have felt not-so-personal, I would love to work with you. If your organization needs an infusion of soul into its people management systems and leadership development, I have methods resulting in rapid transformations on your teams. Now is the time to connect. It is your moment, don't miss it.

***

To contact Molly:

Molly Milinkovich

www.momentlc.com

molly@momentlc.com

612.987.8030

Chad Gaines

Chad Richard Gaines was born on June 3, 1973.

Author and Speaker now. He is widely known for his book, *Who Am I,* and the details of his horrific child abuse when he was a young boy. He spends much of his time doing lectures and coaching on PTSD and the long tern effects. Gaines is now a coach about the concepts of resilience. 2001, His mother killed his stepfather, and he writes the details in his book based on his life "Who Am I" the Chad Gaines story. In 2004, Chad Gaines was honored as one of the Ten Most Outstanding Young Americans (TOYA) in the country. In 2008, Gaines was honored with the Daily Points of Light by President of the United States, George Bush.

In 2020, Hollywood writer Stevie Long wrote the movie script based on Gaines' life. Filming of the movie, Pocket of Hope (The Chad Gaines story) will take place in San Francisco, California in the summer of 2023. Chad had appeared on many podcasts around the world sharing his story and message, Keep Getting Back Up.

The Chad Gaines Story

By Chad Gaines

Every year, more than 8 million Americans suffer from PTSD. Many have done so in silence because of the shame that comes with it. Hi, I'm Chad Gaines and as a young boy, I suffered physical and mental abuse. I know about trauma. I also know about resistance and fighting for life.

PTSD has affected every part of my life. It interfered with all my relationships. My behavior has been at times, out of control as it gets triggered by the events that have happened to me. At one point in my life, my finances were completely embarrassing because of the guilt that I have carried for decades. The guilt of my mother telling me that I didn't deserve any of it and that I was not worthy of any success. I slept on the streets of San Francisco for over a thousand cold nights. However, with those catastrophic events, I learned to cope with PTSD. For me, routine was everything. The key to overcoming PTSD, adversity or challenge, lies in unlocking the transformational power of routine.

In my early twenties, I turned to gangs, hardcore drugs, and became a heavy drinker. PTSD affected my whole being here on earth. I never knew love or what that meant. I soon found myself in a very dark time that led me to prison. Countless nights alone allowed me to reassess my life. I had so many questions. What got me here? Why? What do I want to do with my life? Is this where I want my life to end up at? I slowly found my answers and that's where my life would entirely change. With time and therapy, I learned to understand the triggers of my PTSD. I began to share my story in churches and high schools across America. Through my new mindset, I was able to travel to every state in American sharing my story on stage. I truly believe that the human will to live is the most powerful gift that has been given to us! Eventually I would speak to some of the greatest universities in the country. I was even invited to the White House to be honored for the *Daily Points of Light*. The road has been very long and uneven, to say the least.

Let me explain to you where I was and how I got here writing this to millions of people. I was seven years old when the physical abuse started to affect me. The torture and humiliation I experienced created an unstable man in relationships, in dealing with money & finances, physical insecurities, and a deep, deep depression that nearly took my life more than three times. However, even with suffering those mind-bending events, that wouldn't prepare me for what was next.

Fear took over my thoughts, embarrassment made me feel that I would never be anything in my life. At fifty years young with PTSD, I found it best to control the triggers by having a daily routine to everything. That, and a wonderful *wife* that studies daily to understand my thoughts, feelings, and the huge effects of C-PTSD.

I had a lot of reasons to give up and do nothing with my life. From my early years here on earth, to my teenage drug use, there was no purpose. I failed school. I failed my best friends. I failed my family and I failed myself. I had more than one reason to give up and do nothing. Fortunately, over time I had met many good people in my life, who in turn allowed me to meet other good people in my life. That led me here to write this story that you're reading right now.

In the summer of 2001, I would be twenty-eight years old that morning, when my mother killed my stepfather. At that moment, I recalled that since I was a young boy, she would tell me at least ten times a day that she was going to kill me. And then I realized that it could have been me she killed, instead of my stepfather.

By 2004, I hit rock bottom and that's what saved my life. Just as I was finally clean and sober, then my life was changed forever due to a horrific car accident. During this car accident, my car rolled over nine times, and then once end-over-end landing in a riverbank of ice-cold water. What should have killed me, changed my mindset forever. I escaped the frozen water without a single scratch on my body. The police officers and EMT that night claimed it was a miracle to see me walk away from something so devastating. I knew I was saved for a big purpose. Six months after that horrific car accident, I stood on stage in Tulsa, Oklahoma to be honored as one the *Ten Outstanding Young Americans* in the country for overcoming insurmountable odds.

I would describe life just like a football. It's all about blocking and tackling. You must block the distractions and tackle the opportunities. These skills can be applied to anyone's life. It's an ongoing process that must be yours. College students ask me all the time, "What is the best advice you can give us." I would certainly say the biggest gift I can give you is "Life is going to hurt you!" I give them the hard truth because they deserve to hear the truth.

Life will uppercut you in your mouth. Life will kick you when you're already down and hurting. Life will jab you in the nose many times along the way. It's a fight I tell them. We can't always be soft with our children. Life is hard and it should be explained. If I didn't learn anything from my failures throughout my life, I might not be doing what I'm doing now. We often learn more from our failures than our successes. Is there anyone here who looking back at their past mistakes does not wish they would have done the good and wholesome thing instead of the unproductive one? I tried to remember my failures from my past when I'm on the road, traveling our country, speaking to thousands of people that demand my help at times. It's exhausting at times. It's lonely and it takes time away from my family back home. I found out life is about choices; we all have the same 24 hours in the day. I often perform an autopsy, so to speak, on my own mistakes, there is.

There is no one on earth that is harder on Chad Gaines, than Chad Gaines himself. Sometimes that's what's best for me. Other times, it holds me back from the work I need to do at home and on the road. I always ask myself about once a week, what was my tipping point in my life? I've always attempted to understand where I passed the point of no return. Was it my mom's abuse to me? Was it the drugs and alcohol that I put in my body that should have killed me four times over? Was it losing my best friend at the age of 18? Was it the horrific car wreck that I was able to walk away from? I certainly believe it was a little bit of everything. As Steve Jobs once said, "You can only put the pieces together by looking back at your life."

I've seen enough anguish in our schools through the nation to convince me that evil is real, and death is a regular and frequent intruder on humanity. When I first started speaking in 2000, I was asked to share my journey at a local church in a town where I had hurt so many people. When the youth pastor asks me, I was scared to death. He gave me hope when he told me, "Just believe in yourself." He told me to just wear a suit. Wear a suit I thought? I don't even own a suit and I was twenty-seven years old at the time. I could have given up right then and none if this would be happening for me. I didn't give up. In, fact I walked one mile to a Goodwill store and bought a suit for $15. Three days later, I spoke for the first time in front of 247 people for the first time in my life.

At the end of what I thought was a mess of a so-called presentation, a man would step forward to ask me a question. He was a professor at a *university* and wanted me to share my story at the university. I remember telling him, wherever I'm called to speak, I would go. I wasn't ready for what was about to happen to my life after that encounter with this professor.

I was more frightened because I didn't ask where this university was or how many students might be there to hear me speak. A couple of days later he gave me a call to share the details of the event. I was asked to speak in front of nearly 4,000 students at the University of Norte Dame! Clearly it would have been easy to give up then, but I didn't. At the end, they posted my email address on the digital board to ask others if they wanted to book me as a speaker.

Two weeks later, I received 480 emails from people all over this great country wanting me to speak at their high school and universities. The next thing I knew, I was on a Greyhound bus heading to the middle of Arizona. I had never been to Arizona in my life back then. I can tell you, most of the times, this will never happen. For me, it wasn't luck or good looks I had. It was the day I woke up and knew the two most important days of my life. The day I was born, and the reason why. God simply took my mess and made it a message for millions of people around the world.

I want you to think about a time in your life where you forfeited success, for excuses. If no one has told you that the world is failing because there are more followers, than leaders then you read it here first my friends. Remember that first suit I bought for the $15? Well, I wore that for my first year of my speaking and made over $40,000 in that $15 suit. So don't pretend to be clueless or think you can't do something great in your life with what you have. I've learned to surround myself with people that are growing and not just in height. Again, not an easy thing to do overnight. For my first thirty years of life, I carried the blame for not being able to make my mother and dad feel better about their inner self. To me friends, this is what discovery and recovery is all about! Letting go and letting God handle the messy stuff we don't always talk about. As I reflect on my childhood, I can see how emotionally deprived when I was a young boy and a teenager.

God has certainly given me more than one shot to figure this out. The critics would play it off as I'm lucky or I'm crazy. My life has never been about getting knocked down or knocked out, it about Getting Back Up. Please don't ignore whatever it is your called to do on this planet. Our time here is short as you have read about my experiences. We are simply renting space for a moment. As a man, and a father of a 7-year-old, I can honestly say I believe in you. Every one of you! If I can do what I did. With absolutely nothing., then certainly with all your talent and beauty. You can change a part of the world. If you are wrestling with life's trials., I hope my words empower you to not only want to do more than you're in your life. But to celebrate your victories also. Who better to offer comfort and understanding in times of your trials or grief than someone who has already been through? A similar experience? When you're suffering, would you rather talk to somebody who can speak only about what they heard? And agree with you.? Or would you rather surround yourself? With people who already walked a mile. In your shoes.?

The wonderful people that I now work with Around the country. Are people that I would never dream of even talking to. When I was younger. In 2020, I was approached by a Hollywood writer. That wanted to write my story. As a movie script. I was completely overwhelmed. By the thought. Of 10s of millions of people sitting at home, watching my life story. That I almost *said no*. But what I found was the same challenges that I have been through were the same challenges as the Hollywood film writer had been through in his life. I found a grounding point. Where we could both relate on something, and then he began to write my life story for the big screen. Now I have the great pleasure of sharing just a small amount. Of my story with you and this great book that is filled with incredible leadership, like the winner of the Voice TV show *Craig Wayne*

Boyd! How cool is that a little boy from Kewanna, Indiana, would end up where I am right now in my life! I have a beautiful and loving wife that supports me every step of the way. I have a 7-year-old daughter who keeps me accountable for things that I say and promise others. This is my team. This is my story. I am a warrior.

When I began my search into the Change Book series and discovered the incredible talent that was involved, it was a no-brainer that I needed to be in this book. I truly believe leaders in any business should be in this book! I welcome any of you and all of you to join us on this journey where you can work directly with all of us. I feel it's a wonderful tool to use as there's so much credibility that is attached to this project. I get to work directly with Jim Lutes, who is the author of 13 best-selling books. To be a part of *The Change Book* that will be read by millions, is a bit of fresh air for my family and myself.

***

To contact Chad:

www.gaineschad.com

Chad Gaines | Facebook

Chad Gaines - YouTube

Jonathan Amundsen

Jonathan Amundsen is the founder of Iron Mind Hypnosis.

As hypnotist and owner of Iron Mind Hypnosis he works daily guiding people to the abundant future available to each of us. Jonathan believes that humanity, and many individuals, stand at a fork in the road between death and despair … and a life of health, happiness, and abundance.

As a hypnotist, hypnotherapist, coach, and trainer he uses every skill and experience from years of training, study, work (and even a little living life) to guide his clients to live a life they could barely even imagine. Jonathan is very proud of each new non-smoker with whom he has worked. He is honored to be part of his weight loss clients becoming healthier. And he is flattered when other talented hypnotists seek his help with their problems.

When Jonathan is not working hard to save the world, he is plotting his escape to Mars, excited to raise Martians in a loving community, far from humanity's cradle.

Change as Empirical Science

By Jonathan Amundsen

Is change worth it?

Learning Japanese would be a great idea, even just a little would be good. Now I knew the names of blocks and strikes and not much else. Sensei said I should go to the world karate convention, even as a busy student balancing studies and working to pay for college. So, I added planning a trip and learning another language to my to-do list (not that I actually used lists then). I knew mastering a new language wouldn't happen, but maybe just speaking enough to get around.

If you're not familiar with Japanese and the stats behind learning languages in general, the State Department keeps track of that sort of thing. They end up training a lot of diplomats. They have categories I through IV. This is largely to do with how similar the language is to English. Category I languages like Spanish are "easy," meaning perhaps just 600 hours (24 weeks). Japanese is Category IV "super-hard" ... we are looking at closer to 2,200 hours. That is not a trivial time commitment. Typically, 25 hours a week for 2 years would be plenty. An hour a day for six or seven years would probably do too. Not an hour a week multitasking, working, and studying quantum physics while planning to leave that summer.

So, the first question is, should you even change. Is it worth the time, effort, money, and anything else (friends and family) you will have to give up to make this happen? Otherwise, your change could be how to cope with things the way they are.

Know your why - Feel it

Why that goal? Why Japanese?

For me, I just wanted to be respectful while visiting another country. It wasn't even navigating a strange culture or not getting lost. I didn't want to be obnoxious or entitled. Was that worth trading 2 years of my life for a two-week visit ... maybe not for me.

Every change has a reason why. If there isn't a reason, it simply is not worth any effort to change. (Note: Novelty is a human need, so that can be a reason.) If the reason is not strong and passion-charged, you probably need to simply ask, "why?" There is the rule of thumb of using 5 whys. Asking why you are doing anything 5 times. Why? Then why that answer? For at least 5 levels. Why is it irritating when young children ask why all the time? My guess ... because we don't have good enough reasons, that we can state simply.

In the case of my Japan trip (the second time, when I was wiser), I had just five phrases. The English equivalents are yes, no, please, thank you, and excuse me. No, I don't remember the Japanese words now. The real investment needed was only a few minutes for my true goal.

If your goal was to learn Japanese to impress someone or as a party trick ... juggling could save you about 2,000 hours, plus you could practice almost anywhere. But there are probably hundreds of really good reasons to invest that kind of time in learning a language. It depends on your true goals and situation.

A true goal is that goal at the end of the chain of whys. It is probably something about who you are as a person or how you feel as you go through life. The surface goal is typically just a tactic to achieve that true goal. If the true goal, the ultimate why does not fire you up ... consider doing something else with your life; it is short.

Has this been done before?

Hundreds of millions of people are fluent, and millions of people start Japanese as a second language every year.

Whatever your goal is, find examples of where it has been done. You might have to pull from outside your friend group for this, perhaps outside your industry, specialty, or even country. You want an example to prove that your goal is doable. And, if possible, some hard-won wisdom on how to get there.

No two people are the same, so no two goals or circumstances will be the same. You don't need a clone, but with 7.9 billion people on Earth, someone will be close enough to learn from. In fact, just sharing a birthday with someone who has seen success can make them very relatable. Feel free to use historical figures. But what if your change has never been done before? Welcome to the club!

If your goal is super uncommon or possibly, something nobody has done before, you'll need a rationale for why you are about to do something that several Billion other people just didn't think of or couldn't do.

So why is this thing possible or about to be possible? "Wouldn't it be cool if!?" is not enough. This will probably take some real investment from you. You need a reason to bet a significant part of your life (maybe all of it) that your goal is possible. Many people run away from this step. That can be running away and losing hope or getting high on *hopium* alone without doing careful thinking. You need to check that the physics of your goal will work. Let's be real; the universe is mostly untapped, so stick to things that could fit in this universe.

What if, hypothetically, you wanted to settle on Mars and raise a family, like me? This is a stereotypical example of an unreasonable goal. The sort of thing that you might see in a textbook about therapy. Well, let's run a reality check.

Has it been done?	Nope.
Has something similar been done?	Not really.
Is it banned by physics?	Not that we know of.
Are there examples of parts of this thing?	Yes!

The estimated travel time is about 115 days; is that too long? Humanity has sent a dozen people to the Moon for short stays. The International Space Station has been crewed since 2000. There are 6 people with more than 2 years in orbit.

Can we get to Mars? Well, we have sent a lot of probes. We can soft-land large, complicated rovers with a high success rate these past few years.

What about social factors? Is it possible to keep a group functional in isolated and cramped conditions? Well, there are some mixed results on this, but submarines, fishing vessels, and polar settlements indicate that there is hope.

What about health and reproductive factors? Honestly, we have never kept a human in Martian gravity. Our experience is with Zero and Earth gravity. That's just an example. The more detail you can go into, the better.

Clearly Define your End State

The next critical task is to define what success looks like. What is the end state? Depending on the type of goal, this could be imagining your body in 1 years' time, visualizing your new business either 5 years on or even when you sell it. Your long-awaited vacation, or it might be what it looks like to graduate with that degree or certification.

The clearer your view of what success looks like, the faster and less frustrating the journey will be. And don't worry if there are unknowable variables. You can come through and adjust the goal as needed. But that step should be done deliberately.

Often, people run a success treadmill (also a hedonic treadmill). In both cases, you do stuff and are supposed to be happy, and in neither case are you happy. This is a huge trap. Clearly, defining your end state and stopping to celebrate when you win is so important for further growth. I have heard so many therapists and coaches who have passed their original goals and don't even notice that they are doing well. They might be in a terrible mood when everything is working well. They are ahead of schedule. Pointing out wins is just one really useful job of a mentor or coach.

How can I find Mentors and Good Examples?

Looking for folks who have started where you are and done what you want is a great way to find an example. But that is just the first step. The more examples you have filling the roles of teachers, mentors, and coaches, the better. I have teachers in many areas of my life. We are blessed to live well into the information age; looking up tutorials and basic facts are easier than ever. You can find a "how-to" on almost any topic with a voice search. More information is available with a smartphone than kings or presidents could get even a few years back. It is now too easy to get lost and overwhelmed by all of the conflicting info available. So having one or a small number of voices that have seen success in an area is extremely valuable.

When just starting out in an area, finding a class for the skills you need is usually the first step. This could be a university or trade school in your area or even online. And you might be surprised how many uncommon skills have multiple schools. In my city, I was surprised to discover that there were 3 circus schools. I actually don't know how many of the three had resident performance foot jugglers ... but for a time, one of them had a whole family of resident foot jugglers.

If there is no school, then perhaps there is either a professional or a hobbyist community you can join. You may have to be creative to get this to work, especially if you have a restricted schedule or limited funds. If you cannot find a group or society for your change, you'll want to make a connection with someone who is or has done what you want to do. That could be a close personal friendship in some cases, or it might be reading all the biographies written about a less accessible (or even dead) role model. Ideally, a teacher, mentor, or coach will be the fastest way to get where you are going. Don't waste time DIYing things you don't have to. If this change is important, it may be worth waiting for, but don't wait for it unnecessarily. A teacher usually teaches a skill or set of skills but typically doesn't take a lot of responsibility for how you implement those skills in life. Often these may be large group teaching environments.

A mentor is someone on basically the same path you are, but further along. Get a mentor as soon as you can find a good one and take a mentee as soon as possible. Both giving and receiving will increase your understanding and performance.

A coach is someone who typically takes some responsibility for how you personally perform. It is not just skills lessons to a group, but they guide people in your field to higher performance or toward meeting their goals. A coach may or may not be good at the underlying skill. While it is nice to have a coach who got a gold medal in whatever sport, most great coaches were not actually great athletes. You want a coach willing to stick with you as you troubleshoot a problem or time of low performance.

Metrics - Evidence Procedure

How are you going to know if you are making progress? If you don't have an answer for this, you could be in real trouble. It is possible to head in entirely the wrong direction, guided only by self-delusion. Making great progress and not noticing is a huge problem leading to giving up on working tactics.

A few years back, I was about 80 lbs overweight. I decided to do something about it and changed my meals and reduced calories. I also was getting fairly aggressive with walking. I wanted to lose a nice moderate and consistent 2 lbs per week. But after a short, swift drop on my scale ... the number just didn't move for a couple of weeks. I was getting frustrated and about to get drastic with cutting calories and boosting my walking so that it would have taken over my life. I wanted results ... and I wanted them already.

Fortunately, I had one of those scales that measured weight and body fat percentage, muscle mass, and hydration. (The technology is far from perfect, but it saved me.) I reviewed the tracking in my phone app and was surprised to discover that though the weight number was not budging, I was consistently losing 2 lbs of fat per week, and it was merely being replaced by muscle and better hydration. My results were actually better than I'd hoped for, but I didn't know because I was looking at the wrong number.

In business, this idea is often referred to as Key Performance Indicators (KPIs). They let everyone know at a glance what they are responsible for and how well they are at doing at those things. (KPIs should be a daily or weekly practice ... not a quarterly or annual practice. If you are only tracking things quarterly, you are probably wasting your time.)

The Scientific Process

Hypothesis >>>Test >>>Analysis>>>Report>>>Hypothesis

It is a cycle. Science is not just facts to memorize. There is far more value in learning about how a discovery was made than in just memorizing some facts or narrative.

I used to read books from back to front. I wanted to see how it ended and just memorize facts. (I still kind of do.) But then I'd have to read the book backward all the way to the front to understand the conclusion ... it was just easier not to rush the process.

Hypothesis is the guess. A hypothesis is just a guess of how the world works. As you try to make a change, it is your first guess of how you can do that. Test it! Don't just think you know how to get what you want. Go find out how well your understanding of the world works. Try your plan!

Analysis is how you learn from your test. This is the after-action report or the postmortem. This is where you crunch the numbers, review your journal entries, or read customer surveys. This could be as informal and private as a few sentences in your journal or as formal and public as a scientific journal, newspaper article, or book. Each has its pros and cons.

Report. Yes, strictly speaking, this is optional. You can do science on a desert island or stranded on Mars. If you do this step, it will probably supercharge your results and your understanding.

Hypothesis is just your newest best guess about how the world might work. How you might be able to reach your goals. It is a cycle of testing, analyzing, reporting, and a whole new plan going forward.

Here is something that people often miss. You don't stop just because it either went well or was disappointing. If something improves, you might ask how you can make it 1% better every day or week. Seems trivial, but type 1.01^{365} or 1.01^{52} into a scientific calculator to see what that will do for you in a single year.

There is no failure, only experimental results

It really doesn't matter if you tried to run an experiment, or you just ran an experiment through neglect or distraction ... that data might be valuable.

Like when I analyzed the cake I baked and realized that the eggs were still in the fridge, but the cake was perfectly tasty and moist (if a little crumbly). I just made a good vegan cake that was easier than regular. Or the time I was trying to overachieve with cookies and ended up with biscotti. There is nothing wrong with making accidental biscotti or vegan cake. Or, even, like my housewarming party where the Dutch apple pie I intended turned out ... smokey, so we harvested the cinnamon apples on the inside.

I get it; you need to stay afloat, so it's important to know how risky your next experiment will be. I'm not advocating wild risks. (Harvard was founded in 1636.) I'm advocating a mindset of learning from the results of everything you do try.

Collaboration is valuable

Reporting is part of the scientific method of change. While reporting is optional, it is also very valuable, and frankly, so few people and organizations use it. It is one of the biggest, and easiest to pull, levers for success.

Pearson's Law: "That which is measured improves. That which is measured and reported improves exponentially." – Karl Pearson

There are a couple of reasons for this:

1. Accountability. If you are reporting your work to people who you respect, you will NOT want to let them down.

2. Advice from others working on similar projects can save years.

This isn't about impressing some teachers. It is about getting results.

Research has timelines

I want everything done instantly and perfectly, but that is unrealistic and counterproductive. Important goals need well-thought-out timelines.

The other side of the coin is apathy, not paying attention. Every goal should have a time component. Dates for milestones or tests to be completed or dates to reconsider the project.

You know the tail of the tortoise and the hare. You have been told the tortoise will win, but at some level, you probably still believe you need to make one more heroic effort to fix your life or your business right now. The world keeps pushing you to entertain it with your instant success. But the truth is that not only does the tortoise get where it is going while the hare gets distracted ... or eaten by a hawk. The hare might live to 5 years old. The tortoise might live to 150. You get to choose; it is your life.

***

To contact Jonathan:
Iron Mind Hypnosis
imhypnosis.com
info@imhypnosis.com
206-339-3439

Tammy Goen

As a holistic coach and energy practitioner, I love to help my clients experience "Aha!" moments and move from surviving to thriving. My eclectic approach encompasses skills developed through my previous counseling practice, my 20 years of providing energy healing, certifications in EFT/Tapping and HeartMath Meditation and 8 years as a coach. Throughout the years I have continued to add more self-care and mindfulness practices to my toolbox, which I love to share with my clients.

A Highly Sensitive Person myself, I love helping other HSPs minimize overwhelm and develop a sense of calm, to honor and love themselves and embrace their sensitivities so they become their SuperPower.

There's a way out of overwhelm and struggle, and I help clients on their journeys through a focus on mind, body and spirit to create their new stories and live lives of ease and joy.

Surviving to Thriving: Self Love and the Highly Sensitive Person

By Tammy Goen

Square peg, round hole.

Have you ever felt that you were the square peg, not fitting into a variety of perfectly round holes that everyone else seemed to slide into effortlessly?

If so, there are many potential reasons you had this experience, and one of them could be that you're Highly Sensitive—and it may have been, or still be, a very intense experience. Not fitting in, not being understood, not having the same outlook on life, not wanting what others covet, not being able to let go of concerns and go with the mainstream; just feeling like that square peg.

This was definitely me prior to learning about the trait of High Sensitivity (Sensory Processing Sensitivity). In school and the social arena I always had a sense of looking in from the outside on a world that confused, irritated and pained me. I thought that I should be more like everyone else, that there was something inherently wrong with me, because I was so different. I wanted to fit in, but what I deemed necessary for that just didn't resonate with me.

I had some classic Highly Sensitive Person, or HSP, characteristics and experiences:

I was very good at worrying about others' feelings and needs, to my own detriment. At age 13, my parents having divorced when I was 10, I began to develop stomach aches just before leaving to visit my dad for the weekend. After a few times of seeing this unfold, my mom pulled me aside and asked what was going on. We discovered that I was literally sick to my stomach worrying that my dad was unhappy. I felt his energy and just knew that he was struggling, and I wouldn't allow myself to be happy when he wasn't. As soon as my mom addressed this with my dad and he took responsibility for his well-being, my stomach issues disappeared.

I was perfectionistic and driven to be good and succeed. This made me a great student, but by the time I reached my senior year in high school I'd brought 'putting too much on my plate' to a new, very unhealthy, level. Within a couple of weeks, I was so stressed and anxious about all of the Advanced Placement classes I'd chosen that my mom sat me down again and asked what was wrong. When I explained myself, she suggested I just drop a couple of classes, which I didn't need to graduate, and relax a little for a change. She wasn't disappointed in me or pressuring me to continue since I'd committed—but that is exactly what I was doing to myself. So that year, after following her advice and dropping those classes, I relaxed and spent more time playing racquetball and hanging out with a couple of good friends than studying. What a difference that made.

I felt crushed by many things that happened in the world. One of the most memorable moments in my childhood tv viewing history—and we watched a lot of tv while it rained outside my Portland, Oregon home, was the PSA commercial with a Native American man, a lone tear coursing down his cheek, as he looked upon a river choked with bottles and cans and all variety of human detritus. I seemed to feel the same way—how could people be so thoughtless and unconcerned about their behavior and treat the planet that way? My heart was wounded, and I cried every time I recalled the image. I still see it clearly in my mind's eye, as if it were yesterday, and experience the same feelings.

I was always concerned about what was going on around me. On the bus ride home one day during 6th grade a classmate turned around and stated, "You're such a worry wart Tammy," because I was concerned about someone or something I no longer recall. Of course, I was wondering why she and others wouldn't be concerned, or 'worried'—it seemed obvious that it wasn't ok and something should be done about it. I felt strongly, then and always, the difference between me and everyone else.

In my early adulthood I felt out of place if I wasn't doing something every Friday or Saturday night like everyone else, yet I sometimes actually preferred alone time to hanging out in busy, loud parties or bars or engaging in activities which to me didn't have much meaning. Being busy 'doing' just seemed like what I was supposed to want, but it wasn't satisfying. I wish now that I'd been able to just enjoy that alone time without feeling weird or wrong.

I took great offense to things people did or said in my relationships, feeling slighted or disrespected or unloved, and held onto those feelings for a long time. I grew weary of hearing, "It's not a big deal, why can't you just let it go?"

These are common experiences in the world of highly sensitive people.

The Shift

The turning point in my journey of self-love was the day I discovered an inventory online for High Sensitivity. I knew I was a good person, and I liked who I was, but I always had the feeling that I would need to change myself to be fully ok. The ultimate 'best Me' was based upon comparisons with others. I had no idea how to change, but I kept plugging away at "self-improvement." Taking the high sensitivity inventory—seeing those questions displayed on my screen, changed that in a powerful way.

Learning not only that there was a reason I experienced things the way I did—it's an inborn, genetic trait, but also that I wasn't alone, was the most affirming thing to ever happen to me. Around 20% of the population is Highly Sensitive—a whole community I didn't know existed. There were many others out there who understood what life was like for me, who lived it in a similar way.

I was normal, at least within my minority, and I suddenly was able to reframe my whole past and present and acknowledge that I was fine just the way I am. I didn't need to change myself, to be less sensitive. I just needed some tools to be able to manage in a non-highly sensitive world, and to share my experience with others.

HSPs process everything in life more deeply. We're like sponges with fewer filters and everything is important and meaningful. We see things from all sides, consider the impact on others, have a high level of empathy and compassion, notice all of the little details that others may not even be aware of, think out of the box, feel deeply, connect deeply, tend to have a strong connection with nature and are generally really moved by art and beauty.

What's not to love? Well, other than the overwhelm from overstimulation and feeling drained; being misunderstood and worrying about others; being told we're too sensitive and need to let things go; feeling wrong for wanting a lot of solo time and immersing ourselves in our rich inner worlds; and being affected deeply by the events of the world—not a thing!

It's true—being highly sensitive can be challenging, but by using the self-care tools I already had and developing more, learning more about high sensitivity and how to share it and my needs with others, and coming to honor myself with, not in spite of, my sensitivity, guided me along my path of self-acceptance and self-love.

Using the questions on the inventory helped me to re-evaluate some of my behavior and responses. I now had a better understanding of why I did what I did or felt as I did—what my seemingly unreasonable or inappropriate reactions were all about.

Reading and listening to interviews and podcasts and Ted talks all about high sensitivity were a great first step toward self-acceptance. Being able to normalize is so powerful. Finding HSP-centered articles and webinars reconfirmed that I was part of a community and allowed me to normalize my experiences.

The more I researched high sensitivity and increased my awareness of who I was as an HSP, the more I was able to accept and validate my experience and eventually to recognize the benefits and actually embrace it.

That may seem like a contradiction—'high sensitivity' and 'benefits,' but yes, there truly are many, many benefits to being highly sensitive. As I came to understand and acknowledge this, I began to actually connect with my skills and the positive characteristics of my trait. And I began to see just how my sensitivity helped me in working with my clients.

Surviving to Thriving

But first, what are these benefits? It's really not all struggles. Yes, really.

HSPs are aware of energy and emotion. We tend to know what others need—even how to diffuse potentially frustrating or dangerous situations.

Our high level of compassion leads us to be the ones that others turn to for support, because we listen and understand and offer our hearts. This can be rewarding if we have the right boundaries established.

We tend to be very creative, whether artistically or otherwise. It's likely that your favorite singer or musician, artist or writer is highly sensitive. Our deep feelings come forth in our creativity.

We tend to be caretakers. While that can be detrimental to us if we don't have a solid self-care practice and good boundaries, it also leads us to being great stewards of the planet, voices for the unheard and the abused and neglected and misunderstood.

We experience a deep appreciation of many things in life—we're moved by things that many others don't pay attention to or even notice. Some of us can cry in a moment in response to beauty or a story of great humanitarian acts or accomplishment. We're moved deeply.

We notice little things that others miss, which can keep ourselves and others safe, can help out in challenging situations, or just make our lives so much richer and more vibrant. I liken it to seeing life in technicolor, rather than shades of gray.

We have some deep and meaningful connections. We may not thrive in crowds or enjoy small talk, but we love to talk one on one or in small groups about things that really matter. And it definitely helps to have other HSPs in our inner circle.

There are certainly more benefits. I encourage my clients to make a list of all of the ways sensitivity adds to their life experience, even those which seem initially like challenges or frustrations. For example, I can feel really irritated and distracted by external noises, especially while trying to have a conversation or read or focus on something, but I'm able to notice sounds that others don't and resolve issues before they really become problematic, or they add to my enjoyment of something—like noticing all of the nuances of a beautiful piece of music.

For me this is one of the most powerful aspects of being highly sensitive—the ability to really appreciate and enjoy things in a mindful way. Paying attention to the little details, and acknowledging and enjoying them in the moment, is so rewarding. It also helps us detach from the go-go-go world and immerse ourselves in just being, which is so helpful for our mental and emotional well-being.

And there are ways that our sensitivity benefits us in our work, benefits our coworkers or company or others around us. High sensitivity became my niche in my business once I began to hear from clients that they felt like they could only go so far with their previous coaching or counseling, because they didn't feel truly heard or understood. Being HSP myself, I get it, and it became apparent that this niche was underserved.

Self-Love

So how do we move from accepting our sensitivity and knowing ourselves more, to actually loving and honoring ourselves?

First, we must have a solid self-care practice. If we commit to that, we commit to ourselves. Agreeing that we need a lot of self-care to calm our sensitive nervous systems, and making this a priority without feeling guilty, is a huge step.

We HSPs tend to put others first or want to avoid having anyone be less than happy with us, so we can override our own needs and before long at all, become overwhelmed and exhausted. All humans need to take care of themselves first. Put on the oxygen mask first then reach out to help others, but for HSPs it's even more important.

Next, we need to acknowledge that there's absolutely nothing wrong with being highly sensitive, nothing that needs to be fixed or changed. We can develop tools for managing life in a non-highly sensitive world, and ways to communicate our needs to others, but we don't need to change our sensitivity. Interestingly, when we maintain a regular practice that includes tools for calming the nervous system, we eventually are able to handle more in our environment and feel more in control of our emotions. Everything gets a little—or a lot, easier. We don't become less sensitive; our filters just get more effective.

We also need to identify what is actually already working. Once we acknowledge our trait and accept that some things are actually beneficial, we realize that we're already doing some things really well, things that others might actually struggle with. We need to celebrate those! We need to recognize their value and do more of them.

We often see those things that others complain about as our only characteristics of high sensitivity, but there are many things we do that others love, even depend upon, that they wouldn't want us to change. But that's just normal for us, so we don't always recognize these characteristics as part of our trait, as different. They seem like nothing special—wouldn't anyone else do the same thing? Well, no!

Others likely wouldn't trade your ability to 'be there' for them, to understand what might be going on with someone they have a conflict with, to help them problem solve where they're stuck, to treat them with more kindness and compassion and acceptance than others do. These may come naturally to you, BECAUSE of your high sensitivity. Those are the bonuses we need to celebrate.

And we need to identify all of the things that make us special and stop comparing ourselves to others. Do some people have more bandwidth to accomplish more in a day, or are they able to ignore things that drive us crazy? Sure, but they have other needs that we don't, and they don't experience some of the rewarding things we do, or recognize what situations need that are so obvious to us. We're all just different. We thrive in difference circumstances, different environments, and it's up to us to create those environments that resonate as much as possible.

It's also important to realize that even if someone else seems to have it all together and have unlimited energy for daily life, they might be heading for exhaustion or illness, because they're not taking care of themselves. What's important is identifying and honoring what our own needs are and acting on those, rather than comparing and considering ourselves less-than.

We also need to let go of old thoughts, beliefs and patterns that aren't serving us, that lead us to feel less-than. We are programmed from the first day of our lives—while still in the womb, actually, to think and behave, even feel, in certain ways. Our experiences reinforce these and they become rock solid. While this is great for those things that help us, like looking both ways before crossing the street, others make things difficult for us, like the idea that we need to buck up and let things roll off of our backs.

Shifting our mindset, reframing those beliefs and the self-talk we've carried with us throughout our lives is necessary to embrace fully who we are as highly sensitive people. Everyone has limiting thoughts that need to be confronted and released in order to embrace their authentic selves, but HSPs have the added piece of what we've come to believe it means to be really sensitive, and we need to let those go.

Looking at ourselves through a refined lens that not only allows for our sensitivity, but honors it, allows us to let go of the need to change. I feel so sad when clients or my MeetUp group members say that they just wish they could be not so sensitive, that they could turn it off. I get that, the struggle that can come with being very sensitive, but if we turned it off, we'd miss out on so much of life that we may not realize we're experiencing because of our sensitivity. That's why I help other HSPs to develop good coping strategies and shift their thinking, so they can embrace their trait and allow it to become their superpower.

Life is amazing, and with the right tools and mindset we can fill ourselves with self-love and embrace that life.

***

To contact Tammy:

More about myself and my work, and an HSP inventory, are available at https://coachtammygoen.com/, and links to my social media and some free resources can be found at https://linktr.ee/tammygoen You can schedule a free discovery call here: https://coachtammygoen.com/discovery I'd love to help you along your journey of surviving to thriving.

Afterword

Life is always a series of transitions… people, places and things that shape who we are as individuals. Often, you never know that the next catalyst for change is around the corner.

Jim Britt and Jim Lutes have spent decades influencing individuals to blossom into the best version of themselves.

Allow all you have read in this book to create introspection and redirection if required. It's your journey to craft.

The Change is a series. A global movement. Watch for future releases and add them to your collection. If you know of anyone who would like to be considered as a co-author for a future book, have them email our offices at support@jimbritt.com.

The individual and combined works of Jim Britt and Jim Lutes have filled seminar rooms to maximum capacity and created a worldwide demand.

The blessings go both ways as Jim and Jim are always willing students of life. Out of demand for life-changing programs and events, Jim and Jim conduct seminars worldwide.

To Schedule Jim Britt or Jim Lutes as your featured speaker at your next convention or special event, email Jim Britt at: support@jimbritt.com or Jim Lutes at: mindpowerpro@yahoo.com

For more info on Jim & Jim visit: www.LutesInternational.com or www.JimBritt.com

For information on Jim Britt's online coaching course Cracking the Rich Code: http://CrackingTheRichCode.com

Master your moment as they become hours that become days.

Do something remarkable today! Your legacy awaits.

Blessings,

Jim Britt and Jim Lutes

www.ingramcontent.com/pod-product-compliance
Lightning Source LLC
Chambersburg PA
CBHW070545010526
44118CB00012B/1232